Cistercian Studies Series: Number Two Hundred Twenty-Three

THE LIFE AND MIRACLES OF SAINT MAURUS

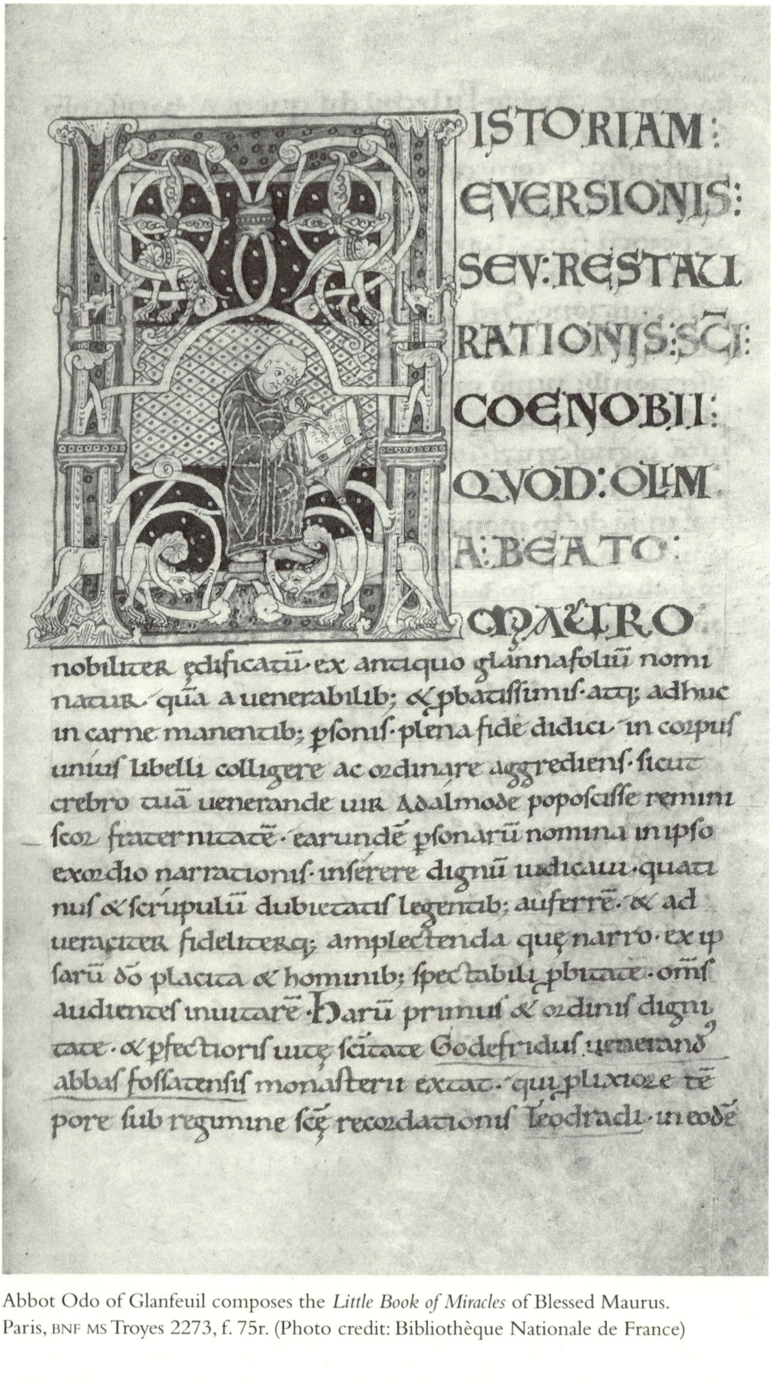

Abbot Odo of Glanfeuil composes the *Little Book of Miracles* of Blessed Maurus. Paris, BNF MS Troyes 2273, f. 75r. (Photo credit: Bibliothèque Nationale de France)

CISTERCIAN STUDIES SERIES: NUMBER TWO HUNDRED TWENTY-THREE

The Life and Miracles of Saint Maurus

Disciple of Benedict
Apostle to France

Translated, with an Introduction,
by
John B. Wickstrom

Cistercian Publications

LITURGICAL PRESS
Collegeville, Minnesota
www.litpress.org

A Cistercian Publications title published by Liturgical Press

Cistercian Publications
Editorial Offices
Abbey of Gethsemani
3642 Monks Road
Trappist, Kentucky 40051
www.cistercianpublications.org

Publication of this book was made possible by support from Western Michigan University to The Institute of Cistercian Studies.

1 2 3 4 5 6 7 8 9

Library of Congress Cataloging-in-Publication Data

Odo, of Glanfeuil, Abbot, 9th cent.
[Life of Maurus. English]
The life and miracles of Saint Maurus / translated, with an introduction, by John B. Wickstrom.
p. cm. — (Cistercian studies series ; no. 223)
Includes bibliographical references (p.) and index.
ISBN 978-0-87907-323-7 (pbk.)
1. Maurus, Saint, ca. 510–584. 2. Maurus, Saint, ca. 510–584—Cult. 3. Benedict, Saint, Abbot of Monte Cassino. I. Wickstrom, John B. II. Odo, of Glanfeuil, Abbot, 9th cent. Little book of miracles. English. III. Title. IV. Series.

BR1720.M36303613 2008
270.2092—dc22
[B]

2008021987

TABLE OF CONTENTS

TABLE OF ABBREVIATIONS

AA SS	*Acta sanctorum quotquot toto orbe coluntur.* Antwerp, Brussels, 1643- .
BHL	*Bibliotheca hagiographica latina antiquae et mediae aetatis.* 3 volumes. Subsidia hagiographica 6 and 12. Brussels, 1898-1911.
DACL	Fernand Cabrol, *Dictionnaire d'archéologie chrétienne et de liturgie.* 15 volumes. Paris, 1907-1953.
MCMA	Herbert Bloch, *Monte Cassino in the Middle Ages*, 2 volumes. Cambridge Massachusetts: Harvard University Press, 1986).
MGH	*Monumenta Germaniae Historica.*
MGH SS	*Monumenta Germaniae Historica.* Scriptores.
PL	*Patrologia cursus completus, series Latina.* Ed. J. P. Migne. Paris, 1844- .
RB	*Regula Benedicti. Benedict's Rule for Monks.*
R Ben	*Revue bénédictine.* Namur, Belgium: Abbaye de Maredsous, 1890- .

THE LIFE OF MAURUS

Above: Saint Benedict casts out a demon. Below: Maurus cures a dumb and lame boy. Rome, Vaticana Latina MS 1202, f. 123r. (Photo credit: Biblioteca Apostolica Vaticana)

HISTORICAL INTRODUCTION

The Origins of the Cult of Saint Maurus

ABOUT THIRTY MILES downriver from Tours on the south bank of the Loire a steep slope rises towards an ancient vineyard. Near the crest stands the small parish church of Saint-Maur-sur-Loire. On close inspection, it becomes evident that the church consists of the nave of a much larger building, now vanished: the monumental abbey church of Glanfeuil. Crowned with four towers, and some two hundred-thirty yards in length, the church formed the core of a medieval abbey that dominated the central Loire valley. Glanfeuil was the proprietor of many outlying churches and farms, but its preeminence flowed from its possession of the relics of Saint Maurus, the first disciple of Saint Benedict and reputed founder of the abbey. After the patriarch and his sister, Scholastica, Maurus was arguably the most revered benedictine saint of the medieval centuries and his renown extended even into modern times. The foundation of the abbey's reputation and prosperity was the famous *Life* of Maurus, composed at the end of the ninth century by the greatest of its abbots, Odo of Glanfeuil. The history of Odo's *Life of Maurus* is, however, anything but straightforward. Its tangled origin reaches back to the days of Pope Gregory I and his famous *Life of Benedict*, written in Rome at the end of the sixth century. Gregory writes that after Benedict had established his first small monasteries at Subiaco, his fame began to attract disciples. Noblemen from Rome brought their sons to Benedict to be trained in the monastic life. Among these was Maurus, the first disciple of Benedict to be identified by name. Gregory tells us that another nobleman's son, Placid, was offered along with Maurus, but 'of the two, Maurus, growing to great virtue, began to be his master's assistant (*co-adjutor*) while Placid was as yet a boy of tender years'.[1] The description is significant because in Chapters Four through Seven of the *Life of Benedict*, Gregory uses the maturing figure of Maurus—and, to a lesser extent, Placid—to illustrate by example rather than abstract principles the monastic virtues Benedict taught.[2] Three different stories are employed to show Maurus maturing from a passive observer of Benedict's power to his active *co-operator*,[3] and to present at the same time important lessons in the progression of christian monastic virtue.

The first of these stories tells of a monk resident at one of Benedict's foundations, who had the distracting habit of wandering about during community meditation. Benedict traveled to the monastery to address the problem, bringing Maurus with him. When Benedict recognized the devil, disguised as a little black boy, pulling the monk about, he

1. *Grégoire le Grand, Dialogues* II, Sources chrétiennes 260 (Paris: Les Éditions du Cerf, 1979) Book 2, Ch. 3, v. 14. Maurus' age at his oblation is given as twelve in the *Life of Maurus*, an age at which many merovingian and carolingian saints typically 'converted' to monastic life: J-C. Poulin, *L'idéal de sainteté dans l'Aquitaine carolingienne, d'après les sources hagiographiques, 750-950* (Québec, Presses de l'Université Laval, 1975) 50.

2. Gregory's principle of illustrating Benedict's teaching by stories rather than in abstract terms seems intended to reflect Benedict's own practice, for, Gregory tells us, 'regarding his [Benedict's] life and conversation, if anyone is desirous of learning more, he may in the instruction of that Rule understand all his manner of life and discipline: for the holy man could not otherwise teach, other than he himself lived': *Dial.* 2. 36. Vogüé sees in these miracles a reference to the three ascending types of scriptural revelation: the law (Moses striking the rock and bringing forth water), the prophets (Eliseus praying that his servant should see and finding the sickle head), and Gospel (Peter walking on the water). *Grégoire le Grand, Vie de Saint Benoît: commentée par Adalbert de Vogüé*, Vie monastique No. 14 (Begrolles-en-Mauge: Abbeye de Bellefontaine, 1982) 66f.

3. Odo of Glanfeuil, *Life of Maurus*, para. 3. For the convenience of the reader, the paragraph numbering and chapter headings for Odo's *Life of Maurus* are adopted from the divisions used in the *Acta Sanctorum* edition: *Vita auctore s. Fausto, AA SS* (Antwerp, 1643-) I:1039-1050. These paragraph divisions are different from those used in the ninth-century manuscript on which this translation is based: Paris, Bibliotheque nationale, MS Lat. 3.

understood the problem to be one of demonic possession. Neither Maurus nor the abbot of the monastery, however, could discern the demon. So Benedict said, 'let us pray to God that you also may see'. After two days of prayer, Gregory says, the demon became visible to Maurus, but not to the local abbot. Gregory makes no further comment on the incident, but his point—the maturation of Maurus in the monastic life—is clear. First, Maurus here begins to share in Benedict's miraculous ability to discern the truth in obscure situations. Second, this story contains hints of petrine qualities in Maurus, an important *topos* in establishing his role as Benedict's successor. Like Peter, Maurus could see spiritual realities to which others are blind.[4]

The second miracle involved a 'poor and devout Goth' whom Benedict had accepted into the community. The novice had dropped the head of a sickle into a deep lake while he was cutting weeds. The Goth ran to Maurus, confessing his guilt. Maurus immediately reported the incident to Benedict, who miraculously drew the missing implement out of the depths and urged the new monk to resume his interrupted work.[5] In this story Maurus is already exercising authority over other monks, functioning as a sort of novice master. Here Maurus is no longer a passive observer of Benedict's power but already his assistant (*adjutor*) in the community.

The evolution of Maurus as Benedict's helper in the monastery culminates in the third of these stories, probably the most famous miracle in Gregory's *Life*. In Chapter Seven, we find that the younger monk, Placid, while gathering water, has fallen into a lake. Although Benedict is a good distance away, he senses Placid's plight immediately and orders Maurus to assist him. Maurus obeys so promptly that he runs over the surface of the lake, pulls Placid to the surface and returns to dry land before realizing that anything unusual has occurred. Gregory highlights the petrine echoes of Maurus' walking on water,

4. Gregory, *Dial.* 2.4.2. See Mt 16:13-19, where Peter alone of the apostles discerns Christ's true identity as the messiah, the Son of God. For examples of discernment as a distinctive virtue of the perfect monk, see Pearse Cusack, *An Interpretation of the Second Dialogue of Gregory the Great* (Edward Mellen Press, 1993) 43, note 5.

5. Gregory, *Dial.* 2.3.14. Benedict's admonition to the novice to continue the work of the monastic day is later echoed in one of Maurus' own miracles, according to Odo's later *Life of Maurus*, para. 43.

describing it as 'a strange thing never heard of since the time of Peter the Apostle'.[6]

A 'friendly contest of mutual humility' between Benedict and Maurus takes place immediately after this rescue. Benedict asserts that Maurus' obedience had worked the miracle, thus exemplifying the famous statement in the Rule: 'they carry out the superior's order as promptly as if the command came from God himself. The Lord says of men like this, *No sooner did he hear than he obeyed me*'.[7] Maurus, on the other hand, insists that the power of Benedict is responsible for Placid's rescue. Despite Maurus' demur, Gregory's text emphasizes his perfect obedience, the supreme monastic virtue of Benedict's Rule. The fundamental lesson here seems to be a test of Maurus' obedience, which, like Peter's faith, is so complete that it results in his ability to walk on water. Unlike Peter, however, Maurus did not falter in his journey over the waves.[8]

This series of three formation miracles shows a clear maturation. Maurus develops from a passive young monk observing the work of his master (in the first miracle of the wandering monk), through competent service as a mediating official in the abbey (in the following story of the Goth's sickle), to a central character acting in perfect obedience to the Rule and his master (in the final story of the rescue of Placid).[9]

Given this *topos* of progress in monastic virtue, Maurus' final appearance in Gregory's life is all the more remarkable. Some time after these events, Benedict, reacting to persecution by a wicked priest, leaves

6. Gregory, *Dial.* 2.7.2. Maurus' imitation of Peter's ability to walk on water in turn becomes the model for a benedictine tradition of this miracle. In the eleventh century, Abbot Desiderius tells the story of a ninth-century abbot of Monte Cassino, a certain Appolinarus, who walked on water 'not only like Christ and Saint Peter, but like Saint Maurus (Desiderius of Monte Cassino, *Dialogi de miraculis sancti Benedicti*, edd. G. Schwartz and A. Hofmeister. MGH SS 30,2 [Leipzig,1934] 1118).

7. RB 5.5, citing Ps 17 [18]:45. Translation: *RB 1980: The Rule of Saint Benedict in Latin and English*, ed. Timothy Fry OSB, (The Liturgical Press: Collegeville Minnesota, 1980) 186 (Latin)-187 (English).

8. Mt 14:22ff.

9. Since oblates provided the major source of monastic populations in carolingian times, the story of Maurus' growth from a young oblate to a perfected monk would have been particularly apposite: Mayke de Jong, 'Carolingian Monasticism: The Power of Prayer,' *The New Cambridge Medieval History* (Cambridge: Cambridge University Press, 1995) 2:640f.

Subiaco to found a new monastery elsewhere. Shortly after Benedict departs, Maurus, who had been left behind, hurries after him with a joyful report that God had struck down the evil cleric. On hearing the news, Benedict grieved deeply, not only because of the priest's death, but because his disciple had rejoiced over it. Benedict then imposes a penance on Maurus for his unseemly elation. For disciples to show less perfection in virtue than their masters is not unusual in hagiographical texts, but Maurus' failure here tends to undercut the earlier theme of his consistent growth in monastic virtue.[10] We may recall, however, that Saint Peter, Maurus' prototype, was also quick to attack his Master's enemies by assaulting the high priest's servant in the garden of Gethsemane.[11] Peter's emotional response earned his Master's rebuke, as did Maurus' later outburst.

The figure of Maurus makes no further appearance in Gregory's *Life of Benedict*. Indeed, he disappears from the historical record for two and a half centuries. Neither Gregory's *Dialogues* nor the *Rule of Benedict* appear to have spread far beyond Rome before the late seventh century.[12] Beginning in the late 700s, however, french abbeys in

10. Such anomalous stories may provide indirect evidence for the historical core of the text: that is, the incident is included because it actually occurred. Such explanations are currently unfashionable since hagiographical texts are regarded as essentially literary rather than historical; such incidents, however, which do not easily fit into a literary or moral structure, are sometimes best explained as a record of an actual historical event.

11. Jn 18:10.

12. An anti-monastic roman clergy deliberately suppressed Gregory's memory after his death, and the Lombards a short time later demolished Monte Cassino itself. Saint Columbanus, writing to Pope Gregory from France in the early 600s, was familiar with the pope's work, and Columbanus' biographer, Jonas, living in northern France in the 630s, perhaps had access to Gregory's *Life of Benedict*: Ian Wood, 'The *Vita Columbani* and Merovingian Hagiography,' *Peritia* 1 (1982) 65, 74. Marilyn Dunn, on the other hand, argues that in the 620s, Columban monasticism was as yet unaffected by Benedict's rule. She casts doubt on the single document suggesting benedictine influence on the Rule of Columbanus by 630, noting that the earliest clear evidence for adoption of the Rule of Benedict in France is at Fleury sometime before 660: Marilyn Dunn, *The Emergence of Monasticism* (Oxford: Blackwell, 2000) 162, 171, 173. Dunn also documents the limited diffusion of Gregory's *Dialogues* almost two centuries after their composition. The work of Francis Clark proposes a radical view of the *Dialogues* as late seventh-century forgeries from England: Francis Clark, *The Pseudo-Gregorian*

ever larger numbers began adopting Benedict's *Rule*, apparently preferring his more moderate regime to that of the irish Columbanus and others, a shift that was encouraged by carolingian church reformers.[13] Gregory's *Life of Benedict* began to spread throughout France along with the Rule.[14] Not surprisingly, the first evidences of a cult of his disciple Maurus appears in France at the same time. Shortly after 800, the prolific carolingian author, Hrabanus Maurus, was given the name of Benedict's disciple by Alcuin because, like the earlier Maurus, Hrabanus had been a happy, successful oblate.[15] In the early 820s, a gallic commentary on Benedict's *Rule* used the argument between Maurus and Benedict over responsibility for Placid's rescue as a model for discussions between monks and their superiors.[16]

Dialogues, 2 vols. (Leiden: Brill, 1987). Although many scholars have attacked the thesis, Dunn's recent survey takes Clark's views seriously: *The Emergence of Monasticism*, 30f. Most feasts of Benedict do not predate the 720s: the earliest celebrations of his cult in France appear to have been at Bourges and Poitiers: John Chapman, 'Apropos des martryologes,' *R Ben* 20 (1903) 298. Kassius Hallinger OSB, 'The Growth of the Cult of Saint Benedict,' *American Benedictine Review*, 36 (1985) 196 admits that 'the *Dialogues* of Saint Gregory were not widely known before 670'. G. Moyse argues that the Rule of Benedict was not used in monastic houses to the exclusion of other rules before the eighth century: 'Monachisme et reglementation monastique en Gaule avant Benoît d'Aniane' in *Sous la règle de Saint Benoît*, Hautes études médiévales et modernes 47 (Geneva, 1982) 8. This controversy, important as it is, does not directly affect the interpretation of the cult of Maurus, since it did not appear until the ninth century. Clark notes that no disciple of Benedict mentioned in Gregory's *Dialogues* enjoyed a saint's cult until several centuries after the work's supposed appearance in the 590s, whereas followers of Columbanus and other early monastic founders had their own cults shortly after their deaths. Clark, *Pseudo-Gregorian Dialogues*, 248-249.

13. Hallinger, 'Growth,' 204. In 743 and 744, frankish synods prescribed the adoption of the Rule of Benedict (Hallinger, 206). In the seventh and early eighth century, french monasteries generally adopted 'mixed' rules in which elements of Benedict's rule along with others were adopted according to local needs and preferences: Moyse, 'Monachisme et reglementation' 5-6.

14. Hallinger, 'Growth' 195ff.

15. 'Rabanus Maurus,' *Catholic Encyclopedia* (New York, 1913) 12:617.

16. Michaelis Smaragdus, *Commentaria in regulam Sancti Benedicti, ad* RB 3.9; PL 102:747. The text is used by Smaragdus to legitimize debates between an abbot and his monks within the monastic precincts. For an english translation, see David Barry OSB, *Smaragdus of Saint Mihiel: Commentary on the Rule of Saint Benedict*, CS 212 (Kalamazoo: 2007) 158.

Most important, around 830, a pious, high-ranking carolingian courtier, Rorigo, Count of Marche and Le Mans, rebuilt and repopulated the dilapidated merovingian monastery of Glanfeuil. Under the direction of members of the Rorigo family, several of whom served as abbots, Glanfeuil became the center of a cult of Maurus during the first half of the ninth century. The Rorigos' activities are recorded in a contemporary history, the *Little Book of Miracles* of Blessed Maurus, composed a half-century later by Odo, abbot of Glanfeuil and a member of the Rorigid clan.

Affixed to the beginning of *The Life of Maurus* is a letter from Abbot Odo to the archdeacon of Le Mans, purporting to recount the discovery of an ancient biography of the famed disciple of Benedict. Odo claims that in the summer of 863, as he and his community fled the attacks of viking marauders, they encountered a group of pilgrims returning from Rome. One of them claimed to have acquired in the course of his travels 'several small volumes' containing *Lives* of Saint Benedict and five of his disciples, including Maurus. Abbot Odo purchased these materials for a large sum of money, but on inspection found the materials to be in a deteriorated condition, written in an ancient and rather blurred hand and 'corrupted as much by an uncultivated style as by the errors of scribes'.[17] In the course of about three weeks, the abbot 'corrected' the *Life of Maurus* from these manuscripts. While he claimed to remain 'faithful to the words and miracles recounted therein', Odo admitted that he 'interpreted and expressed them so that a reader today could understand it all more clearly'.[18]

The resulting text became one of the most influential saint's lives of the Early Middle Ages and was the means by which the cult of Maurus spread throughout western Europe. A lengthy, circumstantial hagiography, the *Life of Maurus* revealed an astonishing tale: contrary to Gregory's account, this disciple had not in fact been left behind when Benedict departed from Subiaco. Rather, Maurus accompanied the master to Monte Cassino. There he so matured in monastic virtue as Benedict's

17. Letter of Odo Abbot of Glanfeuil to Adelmodus in the *Life of Maurus* below, p 60.

18. 'Letter of Odo Abbot of Glanfeuil to Adelmodus,' see below, *Life of Maurus*, p. 60.

cooperator[19] that the master appointed Maurus to succeed him as abbot of Monte Cassino. One day, however, a delegation from the bishop of Le Mans in far-off France appeared at the abbey, asking that a group of monks establish a monastery in his diocese. Benedict acceded and appointed Maurus to lead a small band into France. After an arduous trip through the Alps, punctuated by impressive miracles, Maurus and five companions found the divinely appointed site for their monastery on the south bank of the Loire. There they constructed the abbey of Glanfeuil, where Maurus presided over a community of one hundred forty monks for more than four decades, working miracles and living an exemplary life, until his holy death at age 72 on 15 January 583.[20]

From the time of Abbot Odo until the late seventeenth century, this story of the foundation of a french abbey by Saint Maurus in the late sixth century undergirded a cult of Benedict's disciple that eventually spread to most monasteries of benedictine observance. Beginning with the attack on the *Vita*'s authenticity by the Protestant scholar Jacques Basnage in 1699, historians have increasingly concluded that Odo's 'ancient volume' was not, as the *Life* claimed, the work of one of Maurus' five companions, a monk named Faustus.[21] It was in fact a forgery composed by Abbot Odo of Glanfeuil himself, with most of its details being of Odo's own invention.

Henri Leclercq summed up the arguments for Odo's authorship in a lengthy and still valuable article from 1924.[22] First, the *Life* contains such inaccuracies and unlikely events as to suggest that the author, supposedly an eyewitness, was unfamiliar with the period and topography of the nar-

19. The *Life of Maurus* used the term *cooperator* often (e.g. para. 3, 14, 17) to describe the relationship between Benedict and Maurus and which represented a greater equality than Gregory's description of Maurus as Benedict's *coadjutor*. It is a late latin term that appears first in the New Testament: Phil 2:25 and 3 Jn 8.

20. The name *Glannafolium* indicated perhaps the local hill (*glanna*) and the surrounding woods *folia*, or perhaps a 'shaded riverbank:' See 'Saint Maur' in Célestine Port, *Dictionnaire historique, géographique, et biographique de Maine-et-Loire* (Paris, J. B. Doumoulin, 1874-8) 2:428-430.

21. Jacques Basnage, sieur de Beauval, *Historie de l'Eglise depuis Jesu-Christ*, 2 vols. (Rotterdam, 1699) 2, 1261-1263.

22. Henri Leclercq, 'Glanfeuil' in *Dictionnaire d'archeologie chrétienne et de liturgie* (Paris, 1924-53) 6/1:1283-1319.

rative.[23] Moreover, no copy of the *Life of Maurus* predates its 'discovery' by Abbot Odo, and no other source refers to the details of the story before Odo's lifetime. Finally, more recent work on carolingian hagiography has identified a large group of similar forged biographies of saints intended to legitimate the monastic cult centers of various holy founders.[24] In case after case, late carolingian monastic communities 'discovered' the relics of holy founders, usually from the gallo-roman or merovingian period. They then composed hagiographies of these holy founders, which they often attributed to contemporaries of the saint. These lives often contain an account of an ancient foundation of the cult center by its saint and examples of his patronage on behalf of the monastic community which preserved his relics and promoted his cult.[25] The *Life of Maurus* displays all the essential characteristics of such late carolingian forgeries.

More important, however, for appreciating the significance of the *Life of Maurus* is a recent shift away from arguments over the historical veracity of saint's lives to a discussion of how they functioned within their cultural contexts.[26] The utility of a cult of Benedict's disciple in late carolingian France would have been obvious. Less than fifty miles upriver from Glanfeuil lay the major abbey of Fleury, which had long

23. As examples, the *Life of Maurus*, para. 20f, states that the pilgrims required only two days to travel from Vercelli to Fontrouge, a distance of about one hundred-sixty miles. The *Life* was supposedly presented to 'Pope Boniface' sometime after Maurus' death in 582 (*Life of Maurus*, para. 5), but no pope of that name ruled between 532 and 607. King Theudebert died in 547 and so could not have assisted at the dedication of the monastery church at Glanfeuil in the year 550 as the *Life of Maurus* claimed (para. 47ff.). Moreover, King Theudebert and his successor, Theudebald, were not in control of Anjou and thus could not effectively have granted property at Glanfeuil or traveled there easily as the *Life of Maurus* claims, nor would they have enjoyed the close relationships with the local nobility described in the *Life of Maurus*.

24. The outstanding contemporary investigator of these issues is Thomas Head, *Hagiography and the Cult of the Saints* (Cambridge: Cambridge University Press, 1990). See also Poulin, *L'idéal de sainteté*.

25. For examples of such saints, see Head, *Hagiography*, 7f.

26. In an important article reviewing the last generation of hagiographic studies, Patrick Geary commented, '[T]he positivist concern to separate 'fact' from 'fiction' in hagiography, which gave birth to the great Bollandist undertaking, has largely taken a back seat in modern hagiographic studies'. 'Saints, Scholars, and Society: The Elusive Goal' in *Saints: Studies in Hagiography*, Sandro Sticca ed., Medieval and Renaissance Texts and Studies Series 141 (Binghamton: New York, 1996) 2.

claimed to be the repository of Saint Benedict's bones, translated from Monte Cassino.[27] Moreover, in the early 800s, a cult of Benedict's sister, Saint Scholastica, was also taking shape at Le Mans, another monastic center no more than thirty miles west of Glanfeuil.[28] The monks of Glanfeuil and its restorer, Count Rorigo, surely knew of the wealth and prestige that had come to the abbey of Fleury owing to its possession of Benedict's bones and of the more recent claims of Le Mans, a stronghold of the Rorigo family, to house Scholastica's relics. There is a suggestive parallel between the physical translation of the bones of Benedict and Scholastica from Monte Cassino to french monasteries and the literary journey of Maurus from Italy to the abbey of Glanfeuil in Odo's *Life of Maurus*. Moreover, if it was indeed the high praise of Pope Gregory for Saint Benedict that caused the spread of the latter's cult in carolingian France, then the appearance of a cult of Benedict's first pupil seems to have been almost predictable.[29]

Thus in the mid-ninth century, three abbeys emerged along the banks of the middle Loire, as centers for the veneration of three founding figures of benedictine monasticism. Each produced major hagiographical works demonstrating their abbey's possession of true relics at the same time as the Rule of Benedict was beginning to dominate monastic life throughout western Carolingian France.[30]

The cult of Maurus at Glanfeuil certainly preceded the literary efforts of Abbot Odo to provide a historical basis for its existence. Excavations done at the site in 1898-1899 uncovered an empty coffin in the foundations of a sixth-century circular church built on the ruins of a roman country villa. The remains of this church lie, in turn, beneath carolingian

27. A recent account of the history of Fleury's claim is found in Head, *Hagiography*, 23.

28. The accounts of the translation of Scholastica's bones from Monte Cassino to Le Mans were most likely composed in the mid-ninth century: W. Goffart, 'Le Mans, Scholastica, and the literary tradition of the translation of Saint Benedict,' *R Ben*, 77 (1967) 107-141. It is also noteworthy in this regard that it was the bishop of Le Mans who requested Benedict to send a group of monks to his diocese, *Life of Maurus*, para. 16.

29. Hallinger, 'Growth of the Cult of Saint Benedict,' 204-7.

30. For details on the hagiography of Scholastica in the early ninth century at Le Mans, see note 28 above; for Fleury's ninth-century hagiographies on Benedict, see note 38 below.

and later medieval buildings.[31] Even so, Odo's claim that the cult went back to the establishment of Glanfeuil by Maurus himself in the 550s need not be taken seriously. A more likely origin of the cult is suggested by evidence from another account by Odo, a more contemporary history of the abbey, the *Little Book of Miracles* of Blessed Maurus. There Odo states that, in the reign of Pepin III (751- 768), the flourishing abbey was given over to a lay nobleman, Gaidulf of Ravenna, to be exploited for his private purposes.[32] The monks were expelled and replaced with a few clerics who abandoned the cult of Maurus. The abbey remained in a dilapidated condition for over fifty years. At that point, about 830, while the pious Rorigo, count of LeMans, was searching for a safe refuge where he could adopt a monastic way of life, he received the ruined abbey as a gift from Louis the Pious. There the Count established a strict monastic observance with the assistance of a group of monks sent from the abbey of Fossés in Paris that included his own brother. Once regular life was established, members of the Rorigo family, which included Abbot Odo himself, ruled the abbey until late in the ninth century.[33]

It was probably during the rule of the first of these Rorigid abbots, Gauzlinus, that the cult of Maurus originated or, if it had existed earlier, was significantly strengthened. Odo's *Little Book of Miracles* states

31. Leclercq, 'Glanfeuil,' DACL, col. 1297. The author suggests that a circular structure at the lowest depth was a roman nymphaeum.

32. This practice was common among the earlier Carolingians, before the reforming policies of the late eighth and early ninth centuries: Karl Voigt, *Die karolingische Klosterpolitik und der Niedergang des Westfrankishen Königtums: Laienäbte und Closterinhaber* (Stuttgart, 1917; rpt. Amsterdam, 1965) 53.

33. The exact relationship of Odo to the Rorigo family is uncertain. Odo states that Count Rorigo obtained a royal order stating that a member of 'our progeny' (*progenie nostra*) was to hold the office of abbot of Glanfeuil so long as someone suitable was available: *Little Book of Miracles*, para. 20. Odo seems here to be speaking of his own membership in the Rorigo family. Also L. Levillain, 'L'archichapelain Ebroin,' *Le Moyen Age* 34 (1923) 200. The first Rorigo ruler of Glanfeuil was Count Rorigo's brother Gauzbertus, one of the monks sent from Fossés abbey to reestablish a strict monastic life at Glanfeuil. Gauzbertus did not hold the title of abbot since Count Rorigo had bestowed the abbey on his cousin, Ebroin, bishop of Poitiers. Gauzbertus ruled until 845 then was succeeded by one of Count Rorigo's sons, Gauzlinus, who served as abbot from 845 to 853. His younger brother Theodradus then held the office of abbot until 862 when Odo succeeded him and ruled the community at least until 880. On this issue, see also Voigt, *Die karolingische Klosterpolitik*, 182.

that, at the beginning of his abbacy, Gauzlinus transferred the bones of Maurus to a newer and more elegant shrine. In the course of the translation an old parchment was discovered with the words: 'Here rests the body of Blessed Maurus, monk and deacon, who in the time of King Theudebert came into Gaul and on the 18th of the Kalends of February went forth from this world'.[34] Another reliquary, discovered at the head of Maurus' old burial place, contained relics of Saint Peter, a major patron of carolingian abbeys as well as the New Testament model for Maurus as Benedict's successor. Relics of Saint Stephen were also discovered. As the first deacon, Stephen held the ecclesiastical rank that Maurus would later occupy throughout his life.[35] All these relics were transported to Gauzlinus' newly constructed shrine of Saint Maurus, which thereafter became the cult center of the abbey. It may well be that there was some devotion to Maurus prior to Gauzlinus' abbacy, but the relics were identified as those of Maurus only by this Rorigid abbot, whose 'erudition and learned speech' are emphasized by Odo.[36]

The earliest genuine document that mentions Maurus in connection with Glanfeuil is a charter most likely datable to 839.[37] Henri Leclercq in the 1920s, and more recently Herbert Bloch, both concluded on the basis of the evidence that the origins of the cult of Maurus likely lie in the era of the ninth-century noble Rorigid abbots rather than in the remote merovingian past.[38] It should not be forgotten, moreover, that the documentation and propagation of the cult of Benedict at Fleury occurred about this same time, although his relics had been housed there since the late seventh century.[39]

34. *Little Book of Miracles*, para. 22.

35. Odo states that relics of Saint Stephen were brought from Monte Cassino by Maurus and his companions as a special gift from Benedict *Life of Maurus*, para. 19. Saint Peter was the major patron of the abbey to whom its church was dedicated (para. 46).

36. *Little Book of Miracles*, para. 21.

37. 'Cartulaire de St-Maur-sur-Loire,' *Archives d'Anjou*, ed. Paul Marchegay, (Angers, 1843) 1:326, 'the monastery of Glanna[fueil], where the bodily remains of the blessed confessor of Christ, Maurus rest'.

38. Leclercq, 'Glanfeuil', DACL, col. 1304; Herbert Bloch, *Monte Cassino in the Middle Ages* (Cambridge: Harvard University Press, 1986) 2:971.

39. The major works documenting and celebrating the cult of Benedict at Fleury were produced in the decades after 825 when Adrevauld of Fleury wrote a history

The development of the cult of Saint Maurus from the early ninth century culminated in the two major works by Abbot Odo: the *Life of Maurus* and the *Little Book of Miracles* of Blessed Maurus, both composed in the late 860s. Copies of these works, possibly written by Odo himself, were appended to the so-called Rorigo Bible, an illustrated codex donated to the abbey by its restorer, Count Rorigo. Forced to evacuate his abbey in the face of repeated viking incursions in 863, Odo carried this volume with him, along with the relics of the saintly founder, into exile at the parisian abbey of Saint Pierre des Fossés in 868.[40]

The spread of the cult of Maurus

The important parisian monastery of Saint Pierre de Fossés, where the Glanfeuil community took refuge, provided an ideal center for the spread of the cult because it enjoyed close ties to the carolingian court. Odo was elected abbot of the combined communities in 868 and shortly thereafter composed the *Life of Maurus.* The text, lent and recopied, spread of the saint's cult throughout the north of France during the next century; all subsequent literary and liturgical references to Maurus are based on it. Charles the Bald, the king of West Francia, himself took an interest in the cult, journeying to the new shrine of Maurus in 869, there to pray before the relics and to present the saint with valuable gifts.[41] By the late 900s, Maurus was being commemorated in the liturgy at Chartres and in various norman churches, and this may have in turn influenced the growth of the cult at several centers throughout England.[42] By the year 1000, the abbey of Fleury,

of the translation of Saint Benedict's bones to Fluery, a life of Saint Aigulf who led the expedition to bring Benedict's relics to Fleury, and an influential volume on the miracles of Saint Benedict: J. Wallace-Haddrill, *The Frankish Church* (New York: Oxford University Press, 1983) 350. See also Hallinger, 'Growth of the Cult,' 195-214.

40. That codex, now in the Bibliotheque Nationale as MS Lat 3, was the source for the translation of the *Life of Maurus* below.

41. *Little Book of Miracles*, para. 41.

42. For Chartres, see Réginald Grégoire, 'Prières liturgiques mediévales en honneur de Saint Benoît, de Sainte Scholastique et de Saint Maur', *Studia Anselmiana* 54 (1965) 46. A liturgy of Saint Maurus was celebrated at Canterbury by 1012, at

the major cult center of Benedict in France, had acquired an arm of Maurus. A twelve-lesson office drawn from Odo's *Life* was celebrated at Cluny by the mid-tenth century.[43] By the eleventh century Cluny, too, had acquired an arm of Maurus that was exhibited on feast days, along with imperial insignia given to it by the emperor Henry II symbolizing Cluny's political sovereignty in its neighborhood. Such a juxtaposition perhaps reminded the community at Cluny that Abbot Maurus had demanded independence from his lay benefactors in order to maintain the 'silence and security' of monastic life at Glanfeuil, an example more famously followed at Cluny a half-century later.[44]

For the ever-increasing number of french monasteries which were adopting the rule of Benedict in the late carolingian period, the *Life of Maurus* provided a tradition of observance of the Rule going back to Benedict himself. Cluny's early traditions emphasized this lineage. About 1030, Saint Odilo, fifth abbot of Cluny, prefaced his *Life of Saint Majolus*, (his predecessor as abbot), with a short history of monasticism. It was, Odilo maintained, a continuation of the larger history of salvation which had begun with the preaching of the apostles and martyrs and continued through their successors, the first monks. Later, Benedict gave monasticism a Rule, which he handed on to Maurus, his chosen disciple, who spread it throughout Gaul. This observant monasticism, Odilo claimed, attained an even higher standard through Maurus' disciples until 'through a long span of time that observance rose to the height of perfection'. Thereafter, however, a failure of discipline slowly destroyed the zeal of these founding fathers. This slide into laxity was only reversed, according to Odilo, when Abbot Berno restored at Cluny the monastic discipline of Benedict, Maurus and their followers.[45]

This lineage, traced back to Benedict through Maurus, was revived and refined as a weapon in the polemical battle that cluniac writers

---

Winchester by 1025, and in eight other southern English monasteries by 1060. Francis Wormald, ed. *English Kalendars before AD 1100*, Henry Bradshaw Society, 72 (London, 1934): 30 (Wessex), 100 (Wells), 114 (Hyde), 170 (Canterbury), 198 (Evesham), 212 (Worchester), 240 (Bury Saint Edmunds), 254 (Croyland).

43. Dominique Iogna-Prat, 'La geste des origins dans l'historiographie clunisienne des xie-xiie siècles,' *R Ben*, 102 (1992) 142.

44. A parallel noticed by Iogna-Pratt, 'La geste,' 143f.

45. Odilo V of Cluny, *Vita beati Maioli abbatis*; PL142:946.

waged in the early decades of the twelfth century as they defended black monk traditions against the 'innovations' of Cîteaux and other reformed orders. The *Life of Maurus* was particularly useful in this argument, since for Cluniacs it presented a monastic way of life that faithfully reflected Benedict's intentions as they had been carried into France by his first disciple and chosen successor. The similarities between monastic life at Cluny and that depicted in the *Life of Maurus* were based on the fact that the *Life* was actually composed in carolingian times rather than during the patriarchal age of Benedict, as the cluniac writers assumed.

These parallels were skillfully employed by cluniac polemicists against the supposedly 'authentic' usages of such reformed houses as Cîteaux. In 1125, Abbot Rupert of Deutz compiled the first commentary on the Rule to have been written in three centuries.[46] Concerned to defend the black monks against charges of laxity and excessive wealth, he launched the first full-fledged assault on the cistercian reforming agenda.[47] In Book III of his commentary, Rupert addresses the issues of property ownership and manual labor, which he considered the essential issues separating black and white monk usages. With regard to owing private property, he notes that Maurus accepted property from lay lords sufficient to sustain the one hundred-forty monks of Glanfeuil, adding that, of all abbots, Maurus would be least likely to disregard the spirit of the Rule of Benedict, his 'well-beloved Father'. With regard to the issue of manual labor, Rupert argues that its absence from the monastic life described in the *Life of Maurus* clearly demonstrates Benedict's belief that work should not disturb the leisure of holy contemplation. This, in Rupert's opinion, was the 'proper and highest' activity of monks.[48]

Shortly thereafter in the late 1120s, and again in 1144, the abbot of Cluny, Peter the Venerable, joined in this battle with two famous letters addressed to Saint Bernard. Elaborating Rupert of Deutz's argument, Peter asserts that contemplative prayer was always to be preferred to manual labor. The discipline of Maurus' monastery at Glanfeuil reflected

46. Rupert of Deutz, *In regulam S. Benedicti*; PL 170:477ff.

47. John Van Engen, *Rupert of Deutz* (Berkeley and Los Angeles: University of California Press, 1983) 306, 312f.

48. Rupert of Deutz, *In regulam*; PL 170:515.

this understanding, according to Peter: manual labor was omitted to free the community for 'spiritual work'. Admitting that this represented a change from the Rule of Benedict, Peter nonetheless argues that if it had represented a misunderstanding or perversion of the Rule, God would never have worked such great miracles through Maurus.[49]

Peter finds a still stronger argument to justify the changes from the Rule that characterized monastic life in the *Life of Maurus*. He claims to have found at Marmoutier the autograph copy of Benedict's Rule that the master had given to Maurus as he left for Gaul. Attached to this was a monastic customary known as the *Memorialis qualiter*, which Peter believed to have originated with Benedict himself. The document is, in fact, a carolingian customary, so its usages varied considerably from Benedict's Rule. Unaware of this fact, Peter argues from this document that mitigations of the Rule had already been initiated by Benedict himself and were merely continued by his disciple Maurus.[50]

Orderic Vitalis, a Benedictine of Saint Evroul, elaborated similar themes in Book Eight of his *Ecclesiastical History* (1135). There he puts into the mouth of monks of Molesmes, resisting the incipient cistercian reform, the claim that when Maurus arrived in Gaul, he altered many of the requirements of Benedict's Rule owing to the chill of the climate, which differed from the warm southern atmosphere of early monasticism. Such changes occurred, Orderic argues, because Maurus and other founding fathers of benedictine monasticism wished to encourage monks who could not attain the high standard of early desert asceticism.[51]

Given the use of Odo's *Life of Maurus* as a defence of mitigations from the original Rule of Benedict, it is unsurprising that few early Cistercians mentioned Maurus at all, concerned as they were for the observance of the Rule *ad litteram*.[52] Not until the early thirteenth

49. Letter 28.VII; Giles Constable, ed. *The Letters of Peter the Venerable* (Cambridge: Harvard University Press, 1967) 1:71. For Maurus' modification of Benedict's Rule, see Letter 111; Constable, 1:284f.

50. Giles Constable, *Cluniac Studies* (London: Variorum Reprints, 1980) 125, note 19. Peter removed this valuable document from Marmoutier to Cluny.

51. Orderic Vitalis, *Ecclesiastical History* 8.26; Marjorie Chibnall, ed. and trans. (Oxford: Clarendon Press, 1969-80) 4:316ff.

52. The single exception appears to be Aelred of Riveaulx. In his *Mirror of Charity*, Aelred argued that any provision of the Rule may be dispensed with if the dispensa-

century did a cistercian writer treat Maurus with approval. Tracing the early history of monasticism in his *Exordium Magnum* about 1200, Conrad of Eberbach asserted that Benedict had sent Maurus to establish strict monastic life in France and described Glanfeuil as famous 'both for its observance and its wealth', noting the latter characteristic without the usual cistercian disapproval. Conrad then revived Abbot Odilo of Cluny's argument that, after Maurus' death, observant monasticism continued to spread throughout France until the viking incursions caused it to decline. The first abbots of Cluny, who restored benedictine monasticism to its ancient rigor, in due course reversed this malaise. Over the course of time, laxity gradually entered into Cluny as well, causing Robert of Molesme and his companions to found the New Monastery, where the first Cistercians restored a literal observance of the Rule of Benedict. As a Cistercian of a later generation, Conrad saw the place of Cîteaux in the history of monasticism as less revolutionary than had the twelfth-century founders. For Conrad, Cîteaux was simply another chapter, however glorious, of the ongoing life of monasticism in which Cluny also played a positive role. Therefore Conrad could restore Maurus to an honored place in cistercian history as one of the revered founders of the ongoing monastic tradition in which the white monks now participated.

As the commentaries of cluniac abbots on the *Life of Maurus* indicate, his cult was well known in France from the early eleventh century. Its appearance in Italy, however, occurred later and was closely associated with the revival of the abbey of Monte Cassino in the late eleventh century.[53] Indeed, the appearance of a cassinese cult of Maurus was one of the early signs of the ancient abbey's resurgence after centuries of external invasion and internal disorder. During a

---

tion does not detract from charity and the elimination of vice that was, for Aelred here, the twofold goal of the Rule. For example, he says that Benedict sent Maurus to Gaul despite the Rule's emphasis on stability: Aelred of Riveaulx, *Speculum charitatis* 3.35; PL 195:608ff. English translation by Elizabeth Connor, *The Mirror of Charity*, CF 17 (Kalamazoo, 1990) 281-282.

53. Maurus is not mentioned in eighth- and ninth -century cassinese calendars: G. Morin, 'Pour la topographie ancienne du Mont-Cassin 2: la tour de saint benoît,' *R Ben* 25 (1908) 488. Most of the extant Monte Cassino liturgical calendars of the late tenth and eleventh century commemorate Saint Maurus on January 15th. Grégoire, 'Prières liturgiques,' 51-52.

visit to Monte Cassino in 1028, the renowned abbot of Cluny, Odilo, agreed to transfer to Monte Cassino the arm of Maurus housed at Cluny. The *Chronicle of Monte Cassino* describes the lavish welcome that the returned bones were given. It juxtaposed the sadness of Maurus' departure for France in the flesh centuries earlier with the joy of the return of his relics to his home abbey, where they were ceremoniously placed on the altar of Saint Benedict.[54] About the same time, the liturgical books of Monte Cassino begin to include a commemoration of Maurus.[55]

The revival of the abbey of Monte Cassino reached its apogee in the latter half of the that century under the greatest of its medieval abbots, Desiderius II (1059-1083). Desiderius had planned a reconstruction of the abbey church in magnificent romanesque style. In the course of the excavations for the renovation, he announced the discovery of the bones of Benedict, thereby challenging the claim of Fleury to possess his relics. Shortly thereafter, Abbot Desiderius commissioned a lavishly illustrated lectionary containing both Gregory's *Life of Benedict* and Odo's *Life of Maurus*, arranged as twelve-lesson readings at Vigils on their feastdays.[56]

The illustrated scenes in this important italian manuscript (Vat. lat. 1202) themselves often form novel interpretations of the incidents portrayed in Odo's *Life of Maurus*.[57] In one especially significant example, on fol. 123v (see page 10, above), a pair of miracle illustrations reshaped

54. Odilo's modern biographer claims that this account is much colored by the cassinese chronicler's desire to glorify the abbey and its patriarchs and may not have occurred at all: Jacques Hourlier, *Saint Odilon, abbé de Cluny* (Louvain, 1964) 123.

55. Grégoire, 'Prières liturgiques,' 50-1. Also U. Berliere, 'Le culte de S. Placide,' *R Ben*, 30 (1913) 24. It has been thought till recently that this illuminated lectionary had been commissioned as part of the celebrations for the rededication of the abbey church in 1070 but Francis Newton has been recently argued that the manuscript should be dated some years later: Francis Newton, *The Scriptorium and Library of Monte Cassino* (Cambridge: Cambridge University Press, 1999) 65.

56. Miscellaneous material arranged as lessons for the feast of Scholastica, Benedict's sister, is included as the third part of the codex following the *Life of Maurus* but is not illustrated.

57. John B. Wickstrom, 'Text and image in the making of a holy man: an illustrated *Life* of Maurus of Glanfeuil (MS Vat. lat. 1202)', *Studies in Iconography* 16 (1994) 53-82.

the meaning of Maurus' first miracle, the cure of the lame and blind youth. Odo's text merely stated that Benedict had been called away to perform an exorcism, providing an opportunity for Maurus to work an independent miracle which Odo then described at some length. Desiderius' lectionary, however, illustrates Benedict's exorcism as well as Maurus' cure on the same page. Using these paired scenes, the illustrator emphasizes the distinct status of master and disciple rather than simply showing the first miracle of the latter. The first scene is placed in the upper register of fol. 123 verso, where Benedict stands erect and cowled on the left of the panel, the traditional position of authority, holding the abbatial crozier. He performs the exorcism with his right hand raised in cleansing benediction. The artist places Maurus' cure beneath and to the right of Benedict's, in the subordinate panel. In contrast to the commanding figure of Benedict, Maurus is portrayed bareheaded, bowing down and vested as a deacon, his hands and eyes raised to heaven beseeching assistance. In this way, while Odo's text emphasizes the symbolism of Maurus' first miracle, the illustration features the subordination of Maurus to his master Benedict.

Soon after Abbot Desiderius' death, a series of events in France launched the cassinese cult of Maurus towards the twelfth-century high point of its development. By the end of the eleventh century, Glanfeuil had largely recovered from its physical destruction by the Vikings and its demoralizing failure to recover the relics of Maurus from the abbey of Fossés. For some time, Glanfeuil had been attempting to gain its independence from the parisian abbey of Fossés, which had reduced it to the status of a dependant priory sometime after the death of Abbot Odo. In 1090s, Glanfeuil had appealed the matter to Rome and in 1096 Pope Urban II himself visited the abbey. He released Glanfeuil from the authority of Fossés and granted to its abbot the unusual title of 'cardinal abbot', thereby freeing the abbey from all local ecclesiastical authority.[58] The pope also granted Glanfeuil the right to recover all lands listed as its possessions in the *Life of Maurus*, thereby giving the *Life* a weighty authority.

58. For background on the unusual title of cardinal abbot, see Stephan Kuttner, 'Cardinals: the history of a canonical concept', *Traditio* 3 (1945) 164-165, esp. note 47.

Urban's interest in the abbey shows that by the late eleventh century the cult of Maurus was known and respected in the papal curia. Twenty-five years later, in 1119, another pope, Calixtus II, presided over the dedication of Glanfeuil's rebuilt abbey church. To mark the occasion the newly discovered bones of two holy monks, Constantinianus and Anthony, were solemnly installed in the new structure. According to the *Life of Maurus*, these two had accompanied Maurus on the mission to France. The abbey thereby substituted some reasonably prestigious relics for the remains of Maurus, which the abbey of Fossés had steadfastly refused to relinquish.[59] The chronicler of Monte Cassino records that the monks of his abbey were much involved in these events and were responsible for Pope Calixtus' presence at the new church's dedication.[60]

Cassinese involvement in Glanfeuil was soon to grow as the reviving fortunes of the french abbey brought it to the attention of a new and aggressive bishop of Angers. In the late 1120s, that bishop demanded that the abbey recognized his lordship. In response, Abbot Drogo of Glanfeuil journeyed to Monte Cassino for assistance. The abbot, we are told, traveled with relics of Maurus and a portion of the Rule of Benedict written in the patriarch's own hand, presumably the copy given to Maurus on his departure for France. The abbot's reception at Monte Cassino was described by the abbey's chronicle as a homecoming for Maurus, reviving the theme first entered into its record at the visit of Abbot Odilo of Cluny in 1028.

The address of Drogo to the community of Monte Cassino and its abbot, Seniorectus, on his arrival asserted a 'conjugal' bond between the two houses, noting their intimate relationship (*conjunctio*), and celebrating the 'indissoluble chain of love' between them that had originated in the foundation of Glanfeuil by Maurus, Benedict's disciple.[61] The abbot of Monte Cassino replied with the extraordinary asser-

59. Leo Marsicanus, *Chronica Monasterii Cassinensis* ed. Hartmut Hoffmann (Hannover, 1980) MGH SS 34:527. (Hereafter abbreviated as *Chron. cass*). For the refusal to return the bones, see Port, *Dictionnaire,* 2:420.

60. *Chron. cass.* 793.

61. 'Registrum Petri Diaconi' fol. 253f, printed in *MCMA*, 2:1011-1012. J. F. Niermeyer, *Mediae latinitatis lexicon minus*, 2 vols. (Leiden, Brill, 1976): definition 3 of *conjugatio* is 'vassalage'.

tion that the abbey of Glanfeuil had always been formally and legally bound (*conjugatus*) to Monte Cassino, because it had been founded by the authority (*magisterium*) of Benedict. Glanfeuil should therefore be ruled and protected by Monte Cassino's authority (*imperium*). Abbot Seniorectus then produced a bull of Pope Hadrian IV, dating from 789, that had formally recognized this relationship, along with confirmatory documents from Charlemagne himself, as well as from later popes.

Citing the authority of these documents, Abbot Seniorectus announced that certain rights and obligations flowed to Glanfeuil from its dependency on Monte Cassino: its abbot was formally to visit Monte Cassino every five years. At that visit 'let him hold the place of Maurus and let no abbot sit above him and let him be subject to no house except Monte Cassino'. Abbot Seniorectus then confirmed the supposedly original status of the abbot of Glanfeuil as the *vicarius* of Monte Cassino in France so that 'if issues should arise regarding monastic life in France, they should be settled by the authority of the prior of Monte Cassino and the abbot of Glanfeuil'. [62]

Hearing all this, Abbot Drogo rejoiced and promised obedience to the abbot of Monte Cassino 'just as Maurus had shown to Benedict'. Shortly thereafter Abbot Drogo resigned his office on the grounds of ill health and a member of the community of Monte Cassino, John Marsicanus, was appointed abbot of Glanfeuil by Abbot Seniorectus, who remarked 'however unequal and farfetched it may seem, just as Blessed Benedict sent his venerable disciple Maurus to the regions of Gaul, so he was sending forth Abbot John'.[63]

We now know that the bull of Pope Hadrian and all the other documents establishing the dependency of Glanfeuil on Monte Cassino were forged by Peter the Deacon, the cassinese author of the *Chronicle* of Monte Cassino at this time, in collaboration with Abbot Seniorectus.[64] Peter had a long career of inventing documents that multiplied the rights and privileges of his abbey and even rewrote much of its history.[65] His motives were many and complex, but two of them are

62. Bull of Hadrian I (787) to Abbot Theodemar of Monte Cassino, printed in *MCMA*, 2:1012.

63. 'Registrum Petri Diaconi,' fol. 254, *MCMA*, 2:1014.

64. *MCMA*, 2:990.

65. *MCMA*, 2:979ff.

particularly relevant to the cult of Maurus and the abbey of Glanfeuil. The first was Peter's life-long passion to restore the prestige of Monte Cassino at a time when its influence was in decline. The second was his hostility (and that of his abbey) towards the Cistercians who were replacing the black-monk Benedictines as the most influential and prestigious of monastic institutions. The 'vicarship' of Glanfeuil's abbot over all french monasteries should be understood in this context: the privilege challenged the cistercian domination of french monasticism and in particular, the authority of Bernard of Clairvaux, who was at the height of his influence in the 1130s.[66] Several other conservative monastic writers, such as Peter the Venerable and Rupert of Deutz, were, during the same time, using Maurus as a defence of traditional benedictine customs against the attacks of the cistercian reformers.

In the *Chronicle* of Monte Cassino, Peter the Deacon treated the figure of Maurus, not as a powerful french abbot, but as a saint of Monte Cassino. His stories portray Maurus as having 'come home' to Monte Cassino, where he plays an important role as a powerful protector and patron of his old 'home abbey'. For example, Peter asserts that shortly after King Roger of Sicily had attacked the abbey in January of 1137, Benedict himself appeared to one of the brothers. He announced that the abbey would suffer much because of Roger's aggression but would be delivered through the intervention of Maurus, if the community began to venerate him. From that time on, the *Chronicle* continues, 'every Sunday at the entry to the church after the antiphon of Blessed Benedict, the antiphon of Maurus is recited, and likewise on all feasts in which a collect [of Benedict] ought to be said, just so the antiphon and prayer to Maurus should be said as well'.[67] Shortly after this custom was established, the chancellor of King Roger, who had been harassing the monastery, died suddenly, crying out as he expired, 'Benedict and Maurus, why are you murdering me'?[68] His lament echoes the dying words of earlier oppressors of the abbey of Glanfeuil mentioned in Odo's *Miracles of Maurus* (which Peter had also 'edited'), though there it was Maurus alone who had taken vengeance on the abbey's ene-

66. *MCMA*, 2:993f. Bloch also noted Peter the Deacon's hostility to the Cistercians in his other writings.

67. *Chron. cass.* 563.

68. *Chron. cass.* 564.

mies.[69] Later that same year, Peter continued, a blind old monk named Albertus was celebrating a truce in King Roger's ongoing aggression against the abbey, when suddenly a bright light pierced through his darkness and he could see. He distinguished the figures of two men 'venerable in aspect and dress' at the gate of the monastery, advancing towards him. Together they commanded him to tell the abbot and the community to do penance before the tomb of Benedict. If that were done, God would turn away the dangers threatening the abbey. When Albertus asked who they were, the one revealed himself to be Maurus, 'the disciple of Benedict', and his companion as Placid. The community at once began to perform the penances prescribed before the altar of Benedict's relics.[70]

The prominence of Placid along with Maurus in these stories reflects another of Peter the Deacon's major literary efforts: the creation of a cult of Saint Placid at Monte Cassino. He wrote a brief *Life* of Maurus' young companion under his own name and then forged two other lengthy versions which he attributed to early members of the cassinese community, much as Odo had claimed his *Life of Maurus* to be the work of that saint's contemporary, a monk named Faustus.[71]

Peter the Deacon's hagiographical creativity 'reinvented' Maurus as a saint of Monte Cassino, tying him closely once again to the abbey and to Benedict after Odo's work had loosened that bond by emphasizing Maurus' independence and his role as the founder of benedictine monasticism in Gaul. The widespread devotion to Maurus in benedictine houses in the later middle ages and beyond was in no small degree owing to Peter's reunion of Maurus and Benedict and, to a lesser extent, Placid.

69. Gaidulf, the lay proprietor of Glanfeuil appointed by Pepin III, was killed by a blow from Maurus' staff; the nobleman Witcherius, who later persecuted the monks of Glanfeuil under Abbot Gauzlinus, was similarly dispatched by the saint's power: *Little Book of Miracles*, para. 31. Peter the Deacon knew this document exceedingly well; he had 'revised' Odo's work in order to establish Glanfeuil's dependence on Monte Cassino from its beginnings, providing thereby a foundation for the claims of Abbot Seniorectus in 1130. *MCMA*, 2:977ff.

70. *Chron. cass.* 604-607.

71. The Placid forgeries have been thoroughly discussed by Erich Caspar, *Petrus diaconus und die Monte cassineser Fälschungen* (Berlin, 1909). See R. J. Rodgers, ed., *Peter the Deacon, Ortus et vita justorum cenobii casinensis* (Berkeley, University of California Press, 1972).

Together the three formed a sort of 'holy trinity' of black-monk patriarchs. Yet Odo's *Life of Maurus* remained much more influential in the benedictine hagiographical tradition than did the prolix work of Peter, largely because of Odo's literary elegance and historical persuasiveness.

The cult of Maurus spread throughout the monasteries of Europe in the following centuries, increasingly associated with a cult of Placid and inspiring a large number of liturgical compositions. But no further 'historical' accounts of Benedict's first disciples were composed. By the end of the middle ages, the cult of Maurus and Placid in benedictine houses was second only to the veneration of Saint Benedict and his sister Scholastica.

The *Life of Maurus*
Analysis and Commentary

The *Life of Maurus* can be usefully divided into five major sections:

1. Introduction: Paragraphs 1-6
2. Monastic Youth and Training: Paragraphs 7-15
3. The Mission to Gaul: Paragraphs 16-32
4. The Foundation of the Abbey of Glanfeuil: Paragraphs 33-61
5. The Last days of Maurus: Paragraphs 62-68.

1. Introduction

The material that introduces a saint's life deserves particular attention since it often reveals the author's motives and the underlying ideas of the text.[72] In the *Life of Maurus*, the supposed author, Faustus—in reality, Abbot Odo—first establishes his credentials by relating his own rigorous monastic training by Benedict. 'Faustus' then sets forth his unifying theological theme: the almighty and irresistible will of God. That idea is first elaborated in the central scene of the Introduction: Benedict's vision of the destruction of Monte Cassino after his death. A heavenly voice reminds the patriarch that it is useless to struggle against the will of God but then consoles him with the prophecy that

72. M. Goodich, 'A note on sainthood in the hagiographical prologue,' *History and Theory* 16 (1981) 169.

the glory of the monastery would be restored and that 'the light of monastic life will shine forth from here to other nations'.[73]

This scene served to introduce another underlying thread of the *Life of Maurus*: Glanfeuil in France was the successor of the ruined Monte Cassino as the repository of 'true monastic observance' under the Rule of Benedict. Thus this scene is reprised later in the *Life* when an angel visits Maurus towards the end of his life. Like Benedict before him, Maurus is mourning a divinely-revealed tragedy that seems to negate all he has worked for: most of his monastic community will shortly be carried off by sudden death.[74] Maurus is admonished by the angel—as Benedict had been earlier—not to despair because this event too is in accord with God's will and is, in fact, a great blessing. The lesson to be learned by Maurus in the decimation of the Glanfeuil community differs, however, from how Benedict was to understand the ruination of Monte Cassino: a heavenly messenger had instructed Benedict to trust that the true monastic observance would be carried from the doomed Monte Cassino by Benedict's disciple to France, where it would flourish anew. For Maurus, the lesson appears to be more theological than historical: all men must die, the angel announces to Maurus, but the abbot and his congregation have been given the special grace of a forewarning, allowing them to prepare for their entry into eternal life. This hopeful reminder would have been particularly comforting to Abbot Odo's community-in-exile, in mourning not only over the destruction of their monastery but also over the deaths of their brothers during their flight to Paris in the face of the viking onslaught.

Also of practical value to the community of Glanfeuil in exile was the second and more prominent theme of the Introduction: the presentation of strict observance of the Rule as the chief monastic virtue, a teaching maintained by Maurus personally and carried by him to the new foundation in France. For the monks of Glanfeuil, Maurus' observance of monastic discipline even during a long and arduous journey to an unknown land provided an example and consolation for their own flight into exile.[75] In opening the *Life*, the author prayed

73. *Life of Maurus*, para. 4.

74. *Life of Maurus*, para. 64.

75. The *Life of Maurus* itself (among several others) may have been written in large measure to glorify the relics of the saint in a place of exile. See a similar

that he and all readers of his text might maintain 'the rigor of the monastic life' until death.[76] The author went on to assert that Maurus was chosen for the mission to France because Benedict had trained him 'with strict monastic discipline'[77] in order that he should be second to none 'in monastic observance'.[78] Thus he was prepared to establish in Gaul the same regime. The author returned to this theme repeatedly. First, the promised site of the monastery at Le Mans was taken away by divine intervention as unsuitable for 'zealous monastic observance'.[79] Maurus and his companions were then given more appropriate property by a pious layman, Count Florus, who had been searching for monks 'perfected in monastic observance'.[80] Later the merovingian king, Theudebert, was inspired to grant the monks more extensive lands because they were living 'in holy religious observance'.[81] Maurus demanded total ownership of that property, for the 'observance of monastic life' required the 'greatest quiet'.[82] Count Florus' son, Bertulf, who ultimately succeeded Maurus as abbot of Glanfeuil, was from his youthful entrance to Glanfeuil 'perfected in every sacred monastic observance'.[83] When Bertulf assumed office, Maurus requested the monks who traveled with him from Monte Cassino to remain close at hand and watchful, thereby ensuring that the new abbot maintained 'the correct administration of the Rule'.[84] Maurus spent his final months in solitude, devoting himself to 'the holy way of life of the Rule'.[85] When he observed how the community increased daily in its own 'observant monastic life',[86] Maurus realized his work was

judgment regarding the hagiography of Jumiège in John Howe, 'The hagiography of Jumièges,' *Hagiographie du haut moyen age en Gaul du nord* (Stuttgart, Jan Thorbecke Verlag, 2001) 125.

76. *propositi nostri . . . rigorem.*

77. *religiosissme.*

78. *coenobiali observatione.*

79. *regulari religioni.*

80. *perfectos in hac religione.*

81. *sancta religione.*

82. *observatio ordinis nostri: Life of Maurus*, para. 41.

83. *perfectus in omni sacrosancta . . . observatione.*

84. *rectitudine regularis.*

85. *sancto proposito.*

86. *incrementa sanctae religionis.*

completed; his earthly life ended shortly thereafter. In elaborating this theme of strict monastic observance, Odo's *Life of Maurus* reflects a major theme of ninth-century carolingian religious history.[87] It also highlighted the transfer of the center of benedictine observance from Monte Cassino—still in ruins in Odo's day—to Glanfeuil in Gaul.

2. Monastic Youth and Training

This lengthy section of Odo's *Life* borrows its material from Gregory's *Life of Benedict*, but redirects the emphasis away from Benedict to focus on the monastic education of Maurus. For example, Gregory's references to Placid being offered to the monastery together with Maurus are suppressed while the novel assertion that Benedict loved Maurus 'before all others' is stressed, and a section is added describing Maurus' ascetic practices, a *topos* of carolingian monastic hagiography.[88] The

87. Iogna-Prat, 'La geste' 143ff.

88. Compare the details of Maurus' asceticism with those of the contemporary *Life of Benedict of Aniane*, for example: In Chapter 2, Benedict 'took scanty food, sustaining his body with bread and water to avert death but not hunger, shunning wine as if it were a noxious poison. When his mind was overpowered and he sought a little sleep, he would rest for a short while by lying down on a cheap quilt. Sometimes prostrate on the bare ground, he rested when excessively exhausted, but only in order to fatigue himself even more by such rest. Often spending the whole night in prayer he kept himself awake by standing with bare feet on the pavement in the icy cold. He devoted himself so completely to divine meditation that he would continue many days in sacred psalms without breaking the rule of silence . . . He had a cheap old tunic that he did not change until many days had elapsed. Inevitably a colony of lice grew on his filthy skin, feeding on his limbs emaciated by fasts. His cowls were threadbare with extreme age. When the old thread were finally broken, he patched the rent with any available rag even if of a different color, something that rendered him somewhat unsightly . . . His face grew gaunt with fasting, his flesh was exhausted by privation; his shriveled skin hung from his bones like the dewlaps of cows. Not so much taming a young but ungovernable mind, as mortifying the body, he was compelled by the abbot to exercise rigor against himself more sparingly.' From *The Life of Saint Benedict, Abbot of Aniane*, translated by Alan Cabannis, *Soldiers of Christ*, edd. Thomas F. X. Noble and Thomas Head (University Park: Pennsylvania State University Press, 1995) 219-220. See also *The Emperor's Monk* (Stockwell: Ilfracombe, Devon, 1979) 51; revised edition, *Benedict of Aniane. The Emperor's Monk*, CS 220 (Kalamazoo, 2008) 67-68.

author claims that these austerities had been practiced by Benedict himself, though Gregory's *Life of Benedict* contains few examples of Benedict's asceticism. Maurus carried these out only 'to the degree his father permitted it', and Odo adds that Benedict particularly admired Maurus' love of silence and reading, virtues more in keeping with the benedictine Rule than extreme asceticism.[89] In this way Odo skillfully combined the carolingian preference for monastic asceticism with a focus on Maurus' observance of traditional benedictine virtues.

This section is followed by Odo's retelling of several miracles, drawn from Gregory's *Life of Benedict*, that involved the youthful Maurus. Odo repeats *verbatim* much of Gregory's material, but by adding commentary to the stories, he shifts the focus of the stories away from Benedict's miraculous powers towards Maurus' participation in the events, highlighting in particular Maurus' status as Benedict's disciple and successor. In the miracle of the wandering monk whose demonic possession Maurus recognizes after two days of prayer, for example, Odo adds the comment,'like Peter, he is able to discern, through God's grace, truths that others cannot penetrate'. Odo is here referring to Mt 16:13-19 where Peter's discernment of Christ's true identity was the occasion of his appointment as His vicar on earth.[90] Similarly Maurus was later appointed (in Odo's account) to follow Benedict as abbot of Monte Cassino. To reinforce these images, Odo adds at the end of this story:'Let no one therefore doubt that Maurus was a participant in this miracle, whom his blessed master willed to reveal as the witness and partner (*testem et consortem*) of his great vision and power'.

Odo used a variety of such descriptions to define Maurus' relationship to Benedict. The most common was *cooperator*, a term that appears in the *Life* more frequently than in most other medieval hagiographical texts.[91] The term is used in Odo's work to show that Maurus shares

89. *Life of Maurus*, para. 8.

90. 'Blessed art thou, Simon Bar-Jona: because flesh and blood hath not revealed it to three, but my Father who is in heaven'. Christ then appoints Peter his successor and the 'rock' on which the Church is to be founded.

91. Odo uses the term *cooperator* eight times in reference to Maurus. A search of the *AA SS* database returned the following results for usage of the term: it appears a total of 299 times in 212 *Vitae*. All of these represent one or two usages per text, except for the following: three times in six different texts, four times in three texts, five times in three texts, six times in one text.

in the power and authority exercised by Benedict, and the connotation of reciprocity, or even equality, of the term suggests Maurus' high status as Benedict's appointed vicar.

The second major miracle from Gregory's text in which Maurus participated is the famous rescue of Placid from the lake. Odo rearranged the gregorian material here, placing this event ahead of the incident of the Goth's lost sickle and reducing the latter tale—which included Maurus in a very minor role—to a very brief narrative. After repeating Gregory's narrative of the rescue of Placid virtually *verbatim*, Odo shifts the emphasis of the miracle by adding a long paean of praise by Benedict for Maurus' obedience. Benedict did this, Odo concluded, 'that people would recognize the latter's [Maurus'] holiness by the power of miracles'.[92]

Odo completes his borrowings from Gregory's *Life of Benedict* with a very brief description of Benedict's reproof of Maurus for rejoicing over the death of the evil priest, Florentius, thus glossing over the only incident that suggested any imperfection in his hero.

Maurus disappears entirely from Gregory's *Life of Benedict* at this point. Gregory's implication that Maurus was left behind at Subiaco when Benedict departed to found Monte Cassino presented Odo with a serious difficulty. For the rest of his story to unfold, Maurus needed to be present at Monte Cassino as Benedict's prior and designated successor. For the sake of his own credibility, Odo would not want to contradict the venerable and well-known source he had followed so carefully. He solved this difficulty by neglecting to mention Benedict's departure from Subiaco, and indeed by suppressing the name of Benedict's first foundation entirely. The reader is thereby left with the impression that all of Maurus' early monastic life was spent at Monte Cassino.[93]

At this point, Odo begins to shape an independent narrative of Maurus' later career. Paragraph 33 of Odo's *Life of Maurus* describes a scene set shortly before Benedict's death. The master had been called

92. *Life of Maurus*, para.11.

93. Elaborating on Odo's suggestion, Peter the Deacon's twelfth-century forgery, the *Life of Placid*, states that both Maurus and Placid accompanied Benedict to Monte Cassino and became co-founders with him of that monastery: Pseudo-Gordianus, *Acta Ss. Placidi et Fratrum ejus, AA SS* October 3:117.11.

away to perform an exorcism, leaving Maurus in charge of the community. As Maurus and the monks were returning from working in the fields, they encountered a boy who was deaf and lame. His father and mother begged Maurus to heal him, but the prior refused, stating that he was a sinner and that such miracles 'are the work of the apostles and other perfect men'. But the insistence of the parents, and of the other monks, that Maurus' 'perfection' and 'merits' were sufficient to perform the miracle moved him to action. He prayed that the faith of the first disciples would be visible through his performance of this miracle. He then touched the boy's neck with his deacon's stole, invoking the aid of the Trinity and of his master Benedict. The lame boy immediately stood up on strong, straight limbs. This miracle symbolized the beginning of Maurus' maturation into the one of the 'perfect men', like those of the venerable past he had just invoked. His deacon's stole and his invocation of Benedict's merits, on the other hand, highlighted his still subordinate status.

In order further to emphasize this subordination, Odo fashions the disciple's first cure as a lesser version of a miracle Benedict himself had performed in Chapter 32 of Gregory's *Life of Benedict*.[94] There Benedict and the community were returning from working in the fields when a peasant approached them, begging the holy abbot to restore his dead son to life. As his disciple Maurus later did, Benedict initially refused to act on the grounds of incapacity: 'the holy apostles are the only ones who can raise the dead'.—a comment that has commonly been taken to refer to Peter's raising of Tabitha (Acts 9:36-43). Maurus' cure of the lame boy, however, recalls Peter's first miracle, the cure of a crippled man (Acts 3:1-16). Benedict's raising of the dead child in Gregory's text recalled Peter at the height of his powers; Maurus' cure of a lame child in Odo's work imitated the earlier stage of the apostle's mission. Despite these suggestions of continued subordination while Benedict still lived, Odo's primary emphasis in this story is on Maurus' 'coming of age' as a holy man. Odo underlines this point by commenting that, after Benedict had returned to Monte Cassino and heard of Maurus' achievement, the master would 'no longer think of him in the status of disciple'.[95]

94. Gregory, *Dial.* 2.32.1-3.
95. *Life of Maurus*, para. 15.

3. The Mission to Gaul

With this concluding comment, Odo introduces the next stage of Maurus' career: his journey to France and the foundation of the abbey of Glanfeuil. Shortly before Benedict died, a delegation from the bishop of Le Mans appeared at Monte Cassino, asking that a group of monks be sent to establish 'strict monastic observance' in his diocese. Benedict agreed by means of an address to the cassinese community in which he presented a set of monastic values that were more characteristic of carolingian times than of the days of Benedict himself, when the *Life of Maurus* was supposedly composed.

First, the master stated, Monte Cassino possessed the authentic form of monastic life that would now be spread throughout the frankish kingdom. Second, he would send as head of the mission his chosen successor at Monte Cassino, Maurus, thereby guaranteeing the genuine cassinese character of that life. Benedict also implied that the establishment of observant monastic life in France was of such importance that his most beloved disciple should undertake this mission rather than succeed him as abbot at Monte Cassino. Three parting gifts bestowed on Maurus and his companions by Benedict further underlined this theme of establishing true monastic observance in France: a copy of the Rule written in Benedict's own hand; a balance for weighing the daily ration of bread, and a bronze beaker for measuring out the allowance of wine. Benedict added a warning that these measures were not to be altered.[96]

The handing over of these symbols of authentic benedictine observance, not to mention Benedict's personal authorization of the mission, gave Glanfeuil a claim to primacy and authority over monastic life in Gaul that challenged not only Fleury's preeminence in the carolingian period of the *Life*'s composition, but was later used to counter the claims of the Cistercians to exclusive possession of 'authentic benedictine observance.'[97]

96. Saint Maur des Fossés claimed to possess the brass measure for wine, though another tradition said that the monks fleeing Monte Cassino, owing to the Lombard threat, carried the measures to Rome where they were rediscovered in the nineteenth century: Leclercq, 'Glanfeuil', DACL 1299-1300.

97. See above, pp. 26-27.

Odo describes the journey of Maurus and his companions to France in prophetic biblical language, likening their trek to the wanderings of Abraham, who was given as an inheritance forever the lands to which he came as a pilgrim. Odo also compares Maurus and his monks to Benedict who 'left his homeland desiring only to please God,' and both Benedict and Maurus refer to the expedition as a pilgrimage.[98]

The gradual nature of Maurus' transformation from disciple to master constitutes the central theme of the pilgrimage to Gaul. Its stages were marked by four miracles which Maurus performed along the way. The first of these was the healing of the injured arm of Harderadus, one of the two legates from Le Mans, who was guiding Maurus and his companions to France. Neither Maurus himself nor his companions at first believed him capable of performing such a wonder, and Maurus repeatedly refused his companions' increasingly desperate requests for his intervention. He undertook the task only as a last resort when, after two weeks delay, it became clear that Harderadus' injury would require a painful amputation. Maurus accomplished the miracle by applying a relic of the true cross given to him by Benedict on his departure, and to its merits both Maurus and the cured legate credited the miraculous cure. The narrator thereby highlighted Maurus' continuing dependence on Benedict and the power of cassinese relics for his cures. Shortly thereafter, as the party crossed the Alps, one of the party's servants broke his leg, which Maurus immediately healed by a simple invocation of God's power, with no mention either of Benedict or relics. In the third miracle, Odo begins to identify Maurus' authority with that of Christ by having Maurus reenact one of Christ's major cures: that of a man blind from birth.[99] In his fourth and final cure on the journey, worked just before reaching the monastery of Saint Romanus, Maurus restored to health a widow's son who was near death. It is at this point that Maurus is first given the title 'man of God,' spoken by the widow in gratitude for the restoration of her son. This, the

98. *Life of Maurus*, para. 33. Several writers of the period compared leaving family or fatherland to the wanderings of Abraham. See Jean Leclercq, 'Monachisme et pérégrination du IXe au XIIe siècle,' *Studia Monastica*, 3 (1961) 37. For comparisons of the journey to France to a pilgrimage, see *Life of Maurus*, para. 4 and 33.

99. Mk 8, Jn 9.

most common title given to Benedict by Gregory the Great, had been first accorded to Elijah, Gregory's model for Benedict's *Life*, when he raised the son of a widow in the First Book of Kings.[100] Resurrection miracles were a sign of special holiness, usually reserved to the greatest saints.[101] Yet despite this evidence of Maurus' membership in the ranks of the greatest holy men, it bears notice in this context that the boy had not died, but was 'close to death,' a point that Odo insists on repeatedly, as if still reluctant to place Maurus on a level with Elijah or Christ, Peter, or even Benedict, whose raising of a dead child to life was considered his most important miracle.[102]

The very journey itself was symbolic. It began on the vigil of the fifth Sunday of Epiphany (just prior to Septuagesima Sunday, the beginning of the penitential preparation for Easter in the carolingian period) and reached its climax during the Easter Triduum, with the pilgrims' arrival at a monastery near Auxerre founded by Saint Romanus, Benedict's first guide to monastic observances, according to Gregory's *Life*.[103] Romanus had encountered Benedict soon after he had begun his life as a hermit, clothed him with a habit of 'the holy life' and provided him with food for three years.[104] Odo adds that,

100. For Elijah and Elisha as models for incidents in Gregory's *Life of Benedict*, see Hallinger, 'The Growth of the Cult of Saint Benedict.'

101. Poulin, *L'idéal*, 112.

102. Peter had raised a woman, Tabitha or Dorcus, from the dead: Acts 9:43. For Benedict's resurrection miracle, see Gregory, *Dial.* 2.32.1-3. For its importance, see Cusack, *An Interpretation*, 99f.

103. Gregory, *Dial.* 2.1.6. Though Gregory's dialogue does not specifically mention any master-disciple relationship between Romanus and Benedict, there is a long tradition that asserts such a relationship: Pedro de Ribadeneyra, *Les vies des saints et fêtes de toute l'année* (Paris: L. Vives, 1857) vol. 5:425. At Auxerre, another Saint Romanus enjoyed a cult which Odo apparently conflated with that of Benedict's first teacher: J. Baudot, *Vies des Saints et des beinheureux* (Paris: Librarie Lelouzey et Ané, 1935-1959) 5:425.

104. In commenting on this passage, de Vogüé has suggested that Gregory intended to convey a spiritual 'father-son' relationship between Romanus and Benedict, a bond that—according to Odo—was later formed between Benedict and Maurus. 'By this clothing [of Benedict with the monastic habit] which gave him his birth into the monastic life, Benedict became in some way his [Romanus'] son. By the bread that keeps him alive, he remains in a filial relationship with his father/feeder. Thus the nurse whom Benedict left behind is replaced by this discreet and

later in his life, Saint Romanus had built a monastery in the south of France. Odo inserts this story so that Maurus' mission to France can be understood not only as a lenten pilgrimage—a voyage of dangers and difficulty—but also one of continuing monastic maturation; on Holy Saturday, Maurus was mystically transported from Romanus' monastery back to Monte Cassino where he observed the death and ascent of Benedict, a symbolic final transfer of leadership from Benedict to Maurus, the apostle to France. When Maurus came to himself, he immediately went to inform his companions and Romanus of what had taken place.

That Romanus, Benedict's first companion and *cooperator*, did not witness the master's ascent but was merely informed of it by Maurus suggests that Benedict's first disciple had now replaced the master's first teacher.[105] The final scene between Maurus and Romanus reinforces this suggestion. Romanus announced that nothing would suit him so well as join the mission to France, but advancing age and his sense of impending death precluded this. He therefore merely blessed the pilgrims, predicting lasting success for their labors. Thus did the older generation yield to the new.

4. *The Foundation of the Abbey of Glanfeuil*

Arriving at the cathedral church of Le Mans, the pilgrims found to their dismay that the saintly bishop who had invited them was dead. Worse, his successor refused to hand over the land that had been promised for the abbey. He claimed to be fully occupied with his own plans and with his responsibility for existing churches. This surprising turn of events may reflect the actual ninth-century policy of the bishops of Le Mans that discouraged the foundation of monastic houses.[106] It

---

generous monk,' Gregory the Great, *The Life of Saint Benedict, Commentary by Adalbert de Vogüé*, trans. Hilary Costello and Eoin de Bhaldtraithe (Petersham Massachusetts: Saint Bede's Publications, 1993) 16.

105. It may also be significant that Romanus was replaced by a local priest as Benedict's helper as soon as God had decided reveal Benedict to others: Gregory, *Dial.* 2.1.6. Similarly Romanus is replaced by Maurus when Benedict's teachings are to be spread to France and thereby to 'the whole world'.

106. Head, *Hagiography*, 50

may also show the negative attitude of reformed carolingian monastic writers towards worldly bishops.[107] Finally, Odo's story of Maurus' problems with the bishop of Le Mans may have been intended to legitimize a major shift in the carolingian period that was moving monasteries away from the jurisdiction of bishops and to the protection of the kings.[108] Certainly, Odo dramatically contrasts the indifference of the bishop of Le Mans with the religious zeal of the lay rulers of the region. The primary purpose of this scene, however, was to introduce a major theme of Odo's narrative: the cooperation of the frankish lay nobility with the benedictine monks in the foundation and endowment of Glanfeuil. Thus, immediately after their rebuff by the bishop, Maurus and his companions are invited to stay at the dwelling of Harderadus, one of the former bishop's delegates to Monte Cassino whose arm Maurus had healed during the journey to France.[109] For the only time in Odo's narrative, Maurus has no idea how to proceed, but asks Harderadus for advice. The nobleman immediately suggests a meeting with his nephew, Count Florus, the king's most trusted official in the area. The Count's desire for many years had been to donate to a group of observant, zealous monks a monastery where he could himself enter as a religious, along with his only son, Bertulf.[110] Odo's dramatic account of the first meeting between Count Florus and Maurus is reminiscent of the confrontation between King Totila and Abbot Benedict in Gregory's *Life of Benedict*.[111] As Totila had been, Florus is splendidly arrayed, but on catching sight of Maurus dressed in the humble gown of a traveler pilgrim, he leaps off his horse and prostrates himself. As Benedict had lifted up Totila, Maurus raises up Count Florus and embraces him. But whereas Benedict continued to dominate the scene with Totila, admonishing him for his behavior

107. Poulin, *L'idéal*, 133, 143.

108. De Jong, 'Carolingian Monasticism,' 625f.

109. Harderadus is described as *clericus* though he was married, held extensive lands and high royal offices, and enjoyed a prominent position in the upper aristocracy of Anjou. His role in the narrative is more that of a lay noble than a cleric.

110. Despite his desire for a celibate life, Florus had been married at a young age. His wife had subsequently died, but from this union there had issued a single son, Bertolf: *Life of Maurus*, para. 37.

111. Gregory, *Dial.* 2.15.1-2.

and urging repentance, here the initiative is given to the pious layman, who takes Maurus by the hand, embraces him and, after a long welcoming speech, escorts him into his house. Count Florus then sought the permission of the frankish king, Theudebert, to donate land for the abbey. Once the king was assured that Maurus and his companions were observant monks, he quickly gave his consent. Once again the reader is reminded of the piety of the laity at the highest social levels and of its zeal for the strict monastic life.

This theme of lay piety reappears in a central scene some eight years later, just as the construction of the abbey was completed. When King Theudebert was assured of the rigorous regime that Maurus and the monks observed at the new monastery, he determined to visit the abbey to attend the reception of Count Florus and his son as monks. That this royal *adventus* forms the lengthiest scene in the entire *Life* underlines the importance of the issues it presents. The king first expressed his joy that the wonderful works of Benedict were now being accomplished in Gaul through the person and deeds of his disciple. The king then requested hat his name be inscribed in the community's spiritual fellowship (*societas sua*) alongside those of the monks.[112] The king then introduced his son and heir, Theudebald, to the community, urging him to maintain his father's role as the 'helper and defender' of the community on his succession.

After touring the newly constructed abbey and presenting it with a royal estate and precious objects for the liturgy, Theudebert formally granted Maurus unlimited access to his person. Count Florus then came forward to begin the ritual of being received into religious life. With Maurus and the community arrayed on one side of the altar, the king and his attendants stood on the other side, facing them. The count presented various personal possessions to the abbey and freed several of his servants. He then solemnly laid his sword belt on the altar to signify his withdrawal from worldly affairs. After Maurus had tonsured Florus, at the abbot's behest the king also clipped a few hairs from the Count's head, and he was followed by any of his attendants who

112. Carolingian confraternities of prayer were largely internal monastic institutions until the late ninth century, but royal personages were customarily allowed membership in them: de Jong, 'Carolingian Monasticism,' 649.

wished to do likewise, providing a rare instance of lay participation in clerical tonsure.[113]

The ceremonies of reception ended, Maurus prostrated himself before the king and requested that he enter a building specially constructed for the reception of guests and there enjoy the feast that the monks had prepared.[114] Afterwards Florus, now dressed in the monastic habit, is summoned to stand before the king. Moved to tears of joy at the sight, Theudebert gives thanks for Florus' monastic vocation and admonishes the new monk to surpass his achievements as a laymen. In his monastic life, he must reach ever higher until he attains the very contemplation of God. Having thus instructed his former minister on the spiritual goal of his new life in religion, the king and his retinue depart for Anjou. The *Life* later notes that Theudebert son, Theudebald, and, in turn his successor, Chlothar, both continued to support and revere the abbey as their father had done.[115]

The material support that Count Florus and King Theudebert and his successors supplied to the abbey in Odo's narrative anticipates a pattern that Barbara Rosenwein has documented for the early years of Cluny a century later: land and other donations are made by pious lay nobles out of admiration for the religious life of the monks in return for specific spiritual benefits, such as Masses, membership in prayer fellowships, and burial in the abbey crypt, but without any expectation

113. A few other such incidents of lay involvement in tonsure are known: The lay count Gerald of Aurillac tonsured half his head which he kept hidden: (Odo of Cluny, 'Life of Gerald of Aurillac,' 2:2-3, trans. by Gerard Sitwell OSB, *Soldiers of Christ*, 328). In the seventh century, Saint Ida, mother of Gertrude of Nivelles, tonsured her daughter in order to frustrate the suitors who were pressing for her hand: *Vita sanctae Geretrudis*, ed. Bruno Krusch, *MGH: Scriptores rerum merovingicarum* (Hannover, 1888) 2:456. Tonsure as a part of the formal admission ceremony dates only from the eighth century, a fact that helps to establish the carolingian origin of the *Life of Maurus*: Giles Constable, 'The Ceremonies and Symbolism of Entering Religious Life,' *Segni e riti nella chiesa altomedievale occidentale: 11-17 aprile 1985*, Settimane di studio del Centro italiano di studi sull'alto Medioevo (Spoleto, 1987) 33, 2: 796-797.

114. De Jong, 'Carolingian Monasticism,' 637f, documents the rise of special guesthouses in carolingian monastic houses.

115. *Life of Maurus*, para. 61.

of military or financial assistance.[116] The easy relations of monks and lay lords and their mutual regard in Odo's text also recalls Poulin's observation that, in the carolingian period, the chief religious distinction was not between laymen and monk but between the noble and the non-noble classes. The latter took no part in monastic foundations nor did they participate in the conventional criteria of saintliness itself, which required either clerical standing or noble blood, or, preferably, both of these.[117]

Still, the extent of lay involvement in Glanfeuil's foundation seems extraordinary. Frankish noblemen are depicted not only as material benefactors but as spiritually advanced persons who did not hesitate to lecture a monk on the spiritual goals of the cloistered life and assist in a monastic tonsure, and whose piety even put some clergy to shame. Given Odo's concern for the rigorous observance of monastic life and the preservation of its freedom, his very positive view of neighboring nobility requires some explanation. The cause may lie in Odo's membership in the Rorigo family, the noble restorers of Glanfeuil abbey earlier in the ninth century. Members of his family had served since the 830s as Glanfeuil's abbots. Odo was the last of these, though his precise relationship to Count Rorigo is unclear.[118] We may plausibly conjecture that Odo used the restoration of the abbey by the Rorigos early in the ninth century as a real-life model for his fictive account of its foundation in the sixth century by the merovingian nobility. Just as there was, in the famous phrase of Gregory of Tours, only one 'life of the saints'[119] so, one might suggest, there could be a single ideal 'life of the patrons'. Odo was, of course, intimately familiar with the story of Glanfeuil's restoration, having written an extensive account of it in his earlier work, the *Little Book of Miracles* of Blessed Maurus.

That account of the restoration of Glanfeuil by Count Rorigo shows several remarkable parallels with Odo's story of its original foundation.

116. Barbara Rosenwein, *To Be The Neighbor of Saint Peter* (Ithaca: Cornell University Press, 1989) 38-40.

117. Poulin, *L'idéal*, 127.

118. The exact relationship of Odo to the Rorigo family is never specified in the sources. See L. Levillain, 'Ebroin, évêque de Poitiers,' 200, note 1.

119. Gregory of Tours, *The Life of the Fathers*, trans. Edward James (Liverpool: Liverpool University Press, 1985) 28.

Like the imaginary Count Florus, Count Rorigo was searching for a monastic environment to which he could retire from the world. Just as Odo's merovingian nobles had longed for an observant community and donated the property for its monastery, so Count Rorigo sent for monks from the parisian monastery of Saint Pierre des Fossés to help him re-establish the observant benedictine life at Glanfeuil. Maurus, the saintly sixth-century leader of the founding band of monks, became the first abbot of the community; in the early ninth century the most zealous member of the Fossés monks, Gauzbertus, the brother of Count Rorigo, became first ruler of the restored monastery.[120] Both the fictive sixth-century Count Florus and the real Count Rorigo were said to be buried within the monastery precincts. Moreover, the sons of both of these noble founders become Glanfeuil's abbots: Bertulf, son of Count Florus, and Gauzlinus, the son of Count Rorigo. Both in the narrative of Glanfeuil's foundation in the *Life of Maurus* and in the story of its restoration in the *Miracles of Maurus*, other relatives of the noble founders succeeded these abbots.[121] In both narratives frankish kings are generous benefactors: the carolingian rulers Louis the Pious and Charles the Bald granted lands to the restored Glanfeuil and confirmed its independence, echoing the patronage of the merovingian king Theudebert in the *Life of Maurus*.[122] Finally, Odo's other work, the *Little Book of Miracles* of Blessed Maurus, ends with Charles the Bald's visit to Maurus' shrine after its removal to Fossés in Paris. The king asks the saint's protection for his rule much as Theudebert had done on his visit to the newly established Glanfeuil. Charles also presented gifts for the altar at Fossés much as Theudebert had done at the consecration of Glanfeuil.[123]

While the participation of pious merovingian nobles in the foundation and endowment of Glanfeuil is striking, Odo's text also stresses

120. *Little Book of Miracles*, para. 17, 24.

121. In Odo's 'foundation narrative,' the *Life of Maurus*, the third abbot, Florianus, was the son of Count Harderadus, a noble patron of the abbey and the cousin of Florus, Harderadus' nephew. In the *Little Book of Miracles* the 'restoration narrative,' the third abbot, Theodradus, is a second son of Count Rorigo, the noble restorer of the abbey and the brother of the second abbot, Gauzlinus.

122. 'Cartulaire de St-Maur-sur-Loire,' 326-8. See also *Recueil des actes de Charles II le Chauve*, ed. Ferdinand Lot (Paris, 1955) 3:219-223, 257-260, 354-356, 427.

123. *Little Book of Miracles*, para. 41.

Maurus' insistence on the abbey's independence. Maurus requested that the land which Count Florus donated for the abbey be given 'in full lordship' because 'the observance of our way of life demands the greatest quiet and security'. When Florus agreed, a formal viewing of the property was followed by its formal conveyance into Maurus' 'seigniorial possession' by written deed.[124] Similarly, when Count Florus gave up his remaining lands to the abbey on becoming a monk, he requested that 'a royal edict be made concerning the deed'.[125] King Theudebert 'freely agreed'. When the king later bestowed on the abbey one of his estates, he ordered that the royal recorder of deeds 'should write down the deed for these things and [the king] confirmed it with his signet according to royal custom'.[126]

The author's concern here for written records of land donations may be connected with the fact that Glanfeuil's records of estate ownership, according to Odo, had been lost during the period of oppressive lay lordship over the abbey in the late eighth century and during the viking invasions. The narrative's assertion that such documents had existed could itself be used to support Glanfeuil's claim to ownership of these properties in Odo's day (and indeed, as we have seen, the *Life of Maurus* was later accepted as evidence of land possession by Pope Urban II in 1096)[127]. Moreover, several written charters from later carolingian rulers, which Odo was careful to record in the *Little Book of Miracles*, were confirmations of documents supposedly lost in earlier times of trouble.[128]

Because Maurus feared losing monastic 'quiet and security' from involvement in worldly affairs if the abbey lands formed part of a lay lord's possessions, he insisted on full ownership of the land on which Glanfeuil was built. In a strikingly similar statement, the reforming councils of Aachen in 816-817 had decreed that monastic life should concentrate on prayer, leaving worldly activities to canonical

124. *Life of Maurus*, para. 40.

125. *Life of Maurus*, para 51.

126. *Life of Maurus*, para. 50.

127. See above, p. 29.

128. M. Heinzelmann, 'Studia sanctorum' in *Haut-Moyen Age: culture, éducation, et société*, edd. Claude Lepelley *et al.* (Nanterre, 1990) 141ff.

clergy.[129] Even so, as the stories of the lay nobility's participation in Glanfeuil's foundation clearly illustrate, Carolingian monasteries were much involved with the concerns of their neighbors and local lords. This circumstance necessitated, in Mayke de Jong's phrase, 'a repeated redrawing of boundaries and a renewal of distance'.[130]

Finally, despite the positive light in which lay nobles are depicted, the values of the monastic spirituality that dominated the carolingian period equated secular activities with sinfulness. For example, while the virtuous Count Florus had not wished to marry and desired only to embrace the monastic life, we are told that he nonetheless committed 'many sins' as a result of his secular authority and activity.[131]

Odo's *Life of Maurus* contains a remarkable further comment on the issue which became the locus of controversy in later centuries: holding property. After several years, the number of monks at Glanfeuil had reached one hundred forty. Maurus decreed that this number should never be exceeded 'since the land which now had been granted there sufficed for that number of brothers for those things that were necessary, and if the number were greater possibly it could bring about an occasion of suffering [from lack of provisions]'.[132] This statement was later used by black-monk polemicists in their twelfth-century dispute with the Cistercians regarding the requirement for manual labor: they argued that Maurus' statement indicated that manual labor was not a central element of benedictine life, and that monks could own property (and presumably use laborers) sufficient to supply their needs. Moreover, these polemicists argued, Maurus, as Benedict's first disciple, surely understood and carried out the intentions of his master Benedict in this regard.[133] This controversy and others made the *Life of Maurus* a proof text for genuine benedictine observance among traditionalist writers: what was done at the abbey of Maurus represented the authentic benedictine tradition. This development is of course problematic as Odo's *Life of Maurus* dates, not from the days of Benedict

129. De Jong, 'Carolingian Monasticism,' 629.

130. De Jong, 'Carolingian Monasticism,' 625.

131. *Life of Maurus*, para. 47.

132. *Life of Maurus*, para. 55.

133. John B. Wickstrom, 'Cîteaux, Cluny and Blessed Maurus of Glanfeuil,' *R Ben* 113 (2003) 124-134.

(as was believed until recent times), but from the carolingian period. By that time benedictine monasticism had diverged significantly from what it appears to have been in the time of the founder. Consequently, those unaware of its real date of composition could justify significant changes from early observance, particularly ownership of extensive agricultural land, by appeal to Odo's text.

This lengthy section describing the foundation and endowment of Glanfeuil thus presents a complex picture of the relationship between monasticism and the carolingian world. On the one hand, the lay nobility's zeal for the monastic life exceeds even that of some clerics. Their material generosity to the abbey and their easy access to the cloister all suggest a close bond between the lay and monastic worlds. On the other hand, the insistence on the strict independence of abbey lands looks forward to the age of Cluny. In its attitude towards such matters the *Life of Maurus* is a remarkably transitional document, hearkening back to the 'imperial monasticism' of the high carolingian period, while hinting at the struggle for monastic independence that was soon to come.

5. The Last Days of Maurus

The final days of the founder of a religious community are frequently a focus of hagiographical accounts. The master's central teaching is emphasized in order to perpetuate the original character of the community; the qualities of a successor who will continue these traditions are specified, and the readiness of the founder himself for death provides a model for perfect completion of the religious life he has established.[134] All these topics receive extensive treatment in the last sections of Odo's *Life of Maurus*. Since Maurus and the story of Glanfeuil's foundation is—most likely—a fiction, these final sections in fact represent the views of a late carolingian abbot on the ideal monastic life, and they will be discussed in that context.

134. J. Dalarun, 'La mort des saints fondateurs: de Martin à François' in Jean-Yves Tilliette ed. *Les fonctions des saints dans le monde occidental (IIIe-XIIIe siècle)* (Rome: École française de Rome, 1991) 199f.

This final section opens with the issue of choosing a successor for the abbeys' holy founder. Knowing from a prophecy of Benedict that the end of his life was approaching, Maurus retired to a small cell to pursue a purely contemplative life. At his order, the entire community gathered together and established an unusual qualification for Maurus' successor: he should 'better understand each monk than he understood himself'.[135] The actual choice of Maurus' successor was left to the retiring abbot, a practice that, according to Odo, Benedict himself had followed when he had chosen Maurus to succeed him at Monte Cassino. This abbatial designation of a successor was a common occurrence in carolingian abbeys, despite the Rule's clear requirement of election by some element of the community.[136] Maurus selected the young monk Bertulf, the son of Count Florus, who had been offered to the abbey by his father as a young boy and raised up in the monastic life by Maurus, just as Maurus himself had been trained by Benedict. As a result, Bertulf, like Maurus in the previous generation, became 'the most noble and the most perfected in the monastic life'.[137] In this way, Odo shows the office of abbot passing to a figure who conformed to the carolingian ideal of monastic leadership: a man of virtuous character born of noble blood.[138]

Further to ensure the continuity of observant monasticism at Glanfeuil, Maurus instructed his original companions on the journey to Gaul to remain with Abbot Bertulf so that he might not deviate from the 'path of the Rule'.[139] Maurus then withdrew from the community once again and passed his final two and a half years in solitary prayer and penance. We are reminded here of the last days of his master Benedict. While Pope Gregory did not record that Benedict withdrew into a more intense contemplative life, Benedict's famous vision shortly before his death, in which 'the entire world was gathered up before his eyes in what appeared to be a single ray of light', may have implied such a retreat: for in commenting on this vision, Gregory the Great remarked, 'The light of holy contemplation enlarges and expands the

135. *Life of Maurus*, para. 63.
136. RB 64.1.
137. *Life of Maurus*, para. 63.
138. Poulin, *L'idéal*, 127.
139. *Life of Maurus*, para. 63.

mind in God until it stands above the world. Absorbed as he was in God, it was now easy for him to see all that lay beneath God'.[140]

Gregory had briefly recounted the holy death of Benedict, which occurred shortly after this vision. Odo, however, prefaced his account of the passing of Benedict's pupil with a satanic visitation in which Maurus is attacked for coming into Gaul, Satan's self-proclaimed 'seat of our power'.[141] The devil promised a hellish revenge: most of Maurus' community would soon succumb to death.[142] The incident reminds the reader of the *Life*'s beginning: Benedict's lament over his vision of the destruction of his monastery by invading barbarians. A voice from heaven instructed Benedict not to grieve because the destruction was in accord with the will of God, and men would later be sent forth from the monastery to spread the light of true monastic observance to entire nations. Maurus' dark vision of the future of his community reprises the same theme: an angel informs Maurus that the deaths in his community are the result, not of diabolic power, but of God's will. Moreover this prediction should be a cause, not for sorrow, but for rejoicing, as it will allow the community to prepare for death, which comes to all.

This crisis provides the occasion of Maurus' solemn valedictory to the community. The themes of his final oration are replete with carolingian themes: the salvific efficacy of mortification and prayer; the terrors of judgment and satanic power; and an overall confidence in God's mercy and the expectation of a heavenly reward for monastic fidelity.[143] The speech thus unites the *topos* of a final exhortation to the founder's community and the founder's more personal preparation for his own death. Following on this speech, Odo presents a brief account

140. Gregory, *Dial.* 2. 35. 6.

141. *Life of Maurus*, para. 64.

142. Accounts of the decimation of merovingian monastic communities occur elsewhere in carolingian hagiography and may perhaps refer to the great plague of the sixth century, brought to Italy by Justinian's army. A similar account appears in the ninth-century life of the seventh-century Saint Aichardus: Nine hundred monks and fifteen hundred servants, half of his huge community, died. Like Maurus, Aichardus was forewarned and prepared the monks for the calamity: Howe, 'The Hagiography of Jumièges,' 99.

143. Julia M. H. Smith, 'Religion and Lay Society' in *The New Cambridge Medieval History* 2:665ff.

of Maurus' final illness which closely parallels Gregory's description of Benedict's last days. Like Benedict, Maurus was strengthened at his final hour by the sacraments. Both Benedict and Maurus died surrounded by their community, and post-mortem miracles occurred at the tombs of both the patriarch and his disciple.

Odo of Glanfeuil's *Life of Maurus* is an outstanding example of carolingian hagiography. Set in the remote merovingian past, as was typical of ninth-century saints' lives, it in fact validates the status of a carolingian cult center and illuminates the ninth-century monastic world by its emphasis on relics, monastic asceticism, and independence from lay authority. An outstanding example of medieval monastic literature, Odo's *Life of Maurus* ranks second only to Gregory's *Dialogues* in establishing the tradition of authentic benedictine observance and the saintly qualities of Its holy founders. The blessed Maurus may indeed be a creation of Abbot Odo's imagination; if so, he is one of this creative period's finest fictions. Embodying all the benedictine virtues, Maurus travels through Odo's richly detailed vision of the first days of Benedictine life from Italy into France, an adventure that has been more compelling than any historical reality on which Odo's tale might—or might not—have rested. It is to Odo's story that we now may turn.

Maurus is received into the monastery by Saint Benedict. Paris, BNF MS Troyes 2273, f. 45v. (Photo credit: Bibliothèque Nationale de France)

THE LIFE OF MAURUS

A NOTE ON THE TRANSLATION

The translations of the *Life of Maurus* and the *Little Book of Miracles* that follow have been made from a ninth-century manuscript, 'Odo Glannafoliensis (Pseudo-Faustus), S. Mauri vita et miraculi.' contained in 'Biblia Sancti Mauri Fossatensis seu Rorigonis comitis'. Bibliotheque nationale française. Ms latin 3. fols. 393r-407r. (See Ph. Lauer, *Catalogue général des manuscrits latins*, 7 vols. (Bibliotheque nationale: Paris 1939-) 1:2-3; and BHL no. 5772, 5773, and 5775.

The Carolingian court style of the text features extremely long sentences balanced by briefer statements. The former often differ so significantly from contemporary English usage that a literal translation would sometimes be virtually unintelligible. Therefore, while I have tried to respect the syntax of the manuscript, I have sometimes replaced the complex Latin with shorter sentences and simpler syntax, more in accord with contemporary English usage.

JBW

A Letter of Odo Abbot of Glanfeuil to Adelmodus, archdeacon of the Church of Le Mans concerning the discovery of the Life of the holy Maurus, the disciple of Father Benedict.

ODO, ABBOT of the monastery on the bluff above the bank of the River Loire, which has been called Glanfeuil from ancient times, deeply bound by the chain of holy affection, sends a small gift to Adelmodus, archdeacon of the holy mother church of Le Mans.

You will recall that there has often been conversation between us regarding the discovery of the *Life* of the holy Maurus and of his noble monastic profession, as well as the excellence of his virtues and his deeds. I want to oblige you about these matters, as you have often requested of me and to avoid any frustration that your desire has gone unanswered. So I have resolved to go over everything in writing with complete honesty. It will give me the opportunity to carry out an investigation of this series of events, the likes of which neither I myself nor my brothers have experienced or scarcely even heard of. I much commend your zeal in this matter and your careful enquiry about how we acquired our knowledge of this holy man and what we inherited from him. Let us therefore praise the Father of lights from whom every good and perfect gift comes down from above. We rejoice that this remarkable ornament of all holiness has been welcomed in our region, as you know, through the bishop of the holy see, the most blessed Bertigranus, whom you serve with zeal by God's inspiration.

The savage race of Northmen had laid waste almost all the possessions that remained to us in the neighborhood and, raging, burned them down. Their strength and barbaric cruelty drove us out of our chosen homeland and miserably deprived us of our former habitation, nor did a safe refuge remain anywhere for us. Finally, in a plan designed to save our lives, we decided to make for the territories of Burgundy, carrying the body of the holy Maurus. We came thus to the estate of the illustrious personage, Count Audonus, on this side of the river called the Saône, which he gave to us to live in for a while out of reverence and love for the holy body as well as for an eternal reward. By his kind favor and magnanimous largess, we were allowed to dwell there for a time. So in the year of the Lord's Incarnation 863, in the tenth indiction, we placed the body in a suitable place with befitting solemnity. Then—with the brothers set in order who were attending the sacred treasure with due ceremony insofar as possible—we resolved to set out again for our ancestral soil, free and unimpeded. As we were traversing the nearer banks of the river, we happened on a large party of men of some status. A short while before, they had journeyed to Rome, traveling through the sacred places in order to pray, and now they were hastening on to their homelands. Relieving their burdened beasts, they sat down exhausted from the labor of such a long journey and waited with us on the bank for a vessel. Out of friendliness and wanting to learn about the location and ornamentation of the holy places, we asked many questions and heard many things (as is the case in such matters) about the observance of holiness and piety, about the zealousness of divine worship and attendance at church offices there, about the zeal of Catholics and the exegesis of doctrine. There was a cleric called Peter who, two years before (so he claimed) had journeyed there from the district of Avranches, the place of the holy angel Michael, which is called 'At the Two Tombs'. In his pack there were some small quires, written in an ancient and blurred hand, which had almost been destroyed on account of their extreme antiquity. They contained *Lives* of Blessed Benedict and of five of his disciples, namely Honoratus, Simplicius, Theodorus, Valentinianus, and Maurus. These I was able with some difficulty to purchase for a great deal of money. Because they appeared to be corrupted as much by an uncultivated style as by the errors of scribes, I undertook to correct insofar as I could the *Life* of Blessed Maurus, a task requiring a good three weeks' work. While I remained faithful to the words and miracles reported there, I rephrased and expressed them so that a reader today could understand everything more clearly.

To which, as your persistent interest required, I want to add a little book (*libellus*) about the restoration of the above-mentioned abbey and of the regular observance that was reinstated there, and the wonders that occurred there which many men of high reputation who are still alive vouch for. Through His servant, for the praise and glory of his name, the Divine Majesty deigned to produce both the heavenly visions which had been displayed there by angelic power as well as the wonders worked from the day of his translation up to this hour, both on the road and at the many places where we stopped to rest. Dedicating all this in your name, I judged that it would be useful to readers and of great power for ourselves. I pray, by that truth which is in Jesus, that they will believe what I have published truly and without deceit, so that they might not neglect the requirement of zeal for a more devout life. Thereby receiving on the day of reckoning the fruits of their labor from the Lord, they may deserve to take part in the rewards of eternal life with him whose miracles they are now reading and hearing. Amen.

THUS ENDS THE LETTER

THE LETTER OF THE MONK FAUSTUS, A DISCIPLE OF HOLY FATHER BENEDICT

1. Faustus, servant of the servants of God, to all the monks who live in the north, south, east, and west, and who together with me devoutly maintain faith in the Lord: grace, mercy, peace, and pardon from God the Father almighty, Creator of all things, and from Jesus Christ his only Son, the Lord, our Redeemer and Savior, and from the Holy Spirit, who enlightens and gives life to our souls.

2. At age seven, I had been given by my parents, out of devotion to the merciful God, and to the most blessed Benedict to be reared in the service of almighty God according to the norms of the monastic life within the most holy abbey which that man of perfect sanctity had built on Monte Cassino. It is that devotion whereby God, out of his benevolence, perfects his will and his work in us. He guides us freely by his almighty mercy as we are willing, and by his most merciful grace he follows us, so that the good deeds we attempt to carry out—which he deigns to inspire in us—may not be in vain. How great a thing it is to believe in him with right faith and think on him in goodness and simplicity of heart. Through the gifts he has placed within us, let us hope to receive from him the rewards of eternal joy, if we sustain our faith and sense of purpose firmly and intact to the very end.

Later, as pleased the heavenly Creator, I passed through the years of childhood and then with permission began making use of unfettered study for my improvement. Giving myself intently and completely to understanding the monastic way of life, I wished always to be in the presence of the ever blessed and holy Benedict. With a wholly burning love, I desired instruction in his teachings, which were always pleasing to the Lord and worthy of being followed by men, and I hoped to be strengthened by his shining example.

3. Discerning that in everything I was working diligently at the monastic life and my own salvation, the most blessed father endeavored very frequently to test the steadfastness of my spirit with many subjects, even with propositions he knew to be insupportable and indeed absurd. When thereby he perceived that I was—by the grace of God who wills all to be saved—well prepared and indeed eager to undertake and carefully to complete whatever was needed. He began to make use of my position in his service in preference to others and to instruct me in certain private matters with fatherly affection. He asserted in fact that he had scarcely trusted anyone so completely before, and he secured me as well against tendencies towards vice. Therefore it came about that he assigned me to travel to Gaul along with his disciple, the most blessed Maurus, whom he had also reared and instructed in true monastic discipline, and who by the merit of his way of life and the excellence of his virtues had become the co-worker (*cooperator*) of the master. To him [Maurus] I provided some comfort by abiding with him, and in the end I was the sole survivor from among those first students who had been instructed by Benedict and then sent to those remote foreign regions to establish the foundations of monastic life.

4. The omnipotent majesty of divinity, surrounding and interpenetrating everything, understands thoughts from afar and knows all things, from ancient to the most recent and foresees the paths of every person. Therefore God revealed to the most holy father that the monastery which he himself had built in that lofty place would be destroyed and demolished by his inscrutable judgment. Inconsolably affected at this, the man of the Lord wept continuously over this affliction, so to comfort him a revelation was granted by the following oracle: 'Most honorable Benedict, most beloved of God, do not agitate your spirit over what you have learned shall befall this place. What has been once decreed by the inscrutable decision of the Deity will unchangeably and irrevocably be accomplished. Owing to your merit, the souls of all those dwelling herein have been entrusted to you alone and the gracious consolation of the Almighty will be present here as in times past. Owing to your merits as well, he shall restore the monastery to its pristine rank, indeed even higher, than it now appears. Moreover the light of monastic observance will shine forth from here to other nations.

One day more worthy and well-seasoned men shall make up the flock of this monastery, and then you will be asked, indeed entreated, to send them forth. The abundant fruit of their labor will surely be added to the sum of rewards you will receive, and it will guide them into the dwelling place of everlasting blessedness.' Thus it was that our most holy Father, beloved of God, was reassured by the oracle and as he shortly thereafter had met with a legation from the bishop of Le Mans asking for assistance, the most holy father, beloved of God, immediately summoned Maurus, the perfectly observant monk, and—with the assent of the whole congregation—entrusted him to the bishop's legates. He then assigned Simplicius, Antony, and Constantinianus to be his companions and fellow-workers (*cooperatores*). Myself as well he appointed as a follower in their labor and pilgrimage—though not of their wholly excellent deeds.

5. Long after the passing of that distinguished confessor of Christ, Benedict our teacher and worker of wondrous deeds, and after the most blessed Maurus and our two companions, Constantinianus and Antony, had also been long since buried, I returned to our monastery, together with Simplicius, as Blessed Maurus had ordered, having lived almost an entire lifetime. Urged on by all the brothers of the monastery of Monte Cassino, whence we had gone forth, and especially by that most observant monk fittingly named Theodorus, who had for a long time ruled over the congregation of the monastery of the Lateran (the third after Valentinianus of holy memory), I undertook to write a history of the life and monastic deportment of the most blessed Maurus; I described his departure and the raising of the monastery which with God's help he built well and elegantly. I wrote too of the miracles which the Lord willed to work through his servant to the praise and glory of His name. These things occurred among us, and we saw them with our own eyes, recalling the more remote events and even those from the time of his birth. I myself advise no one to doubt the truth of this narrative and its deeds, for I am quite aware that it is better to remain silent than to narrate something that is frivolous or fictional. Finally, I myself showed this little work to the most blessed Pope Boniface: the holy pontiff approving the work, deemed it praiseworthy and validated it by his sacred authority.

6. I beseech all those who take this book up to read not to be put off by its rustic and unlearned style but rather to be forgiving. I may be thought adept in none of the conventions of the literary profession by which I might be supported, but I would not allow those deeds which the Lord accomplished through his servant, at which I myself was present, to be hidden in silence. I was especially compelled to write these events down, however I could, not only by brotherly love and entreaties but by the command of holy men which I could not ignore.

CHAPTER ONE: THE INSTRUCTION OF BLESSED MAURUS THE ZEAL OF HIS PENANCES

7. The divinity of Our Lord and Savior Jesus Christ, shining forth in his miracles performed in the flesh, condescended to save the human race. This was revealed to the whole world through the preaching of the Apostles. Redeemed by the most holy blood of its Lord, the Catholic Church was consecrated in the blood of innumerable martyrs who, crowned victorious by their suffering, have left to the weaker souls who followed the easier discipline of faith. The loftiness of the imperial dignity itself, once proud and worldly, was also brought under the yoke of faith through the kindness and mercy of the Creator and Deliverer of all and by the law of a most merciful and rational justice. After all this, through God's providence, many holy men appeared far and wide. Strengthened by divine assistance, and fighting manfully against the prince of this world, they renounced the allurements of the body and the delights of the flesh in a desire for eternal rewards. As mighty in the power of their miracles as brilliant in their knowledge of spiritual teaching, they became as well most zealous in performing good deeds, and from their appearance down to our own times, they shine alike in memory and in the reading of ancient memorials. Among them, in the days of Justin and Childeric, king of the Vandals, glowing like the brightest of all the stars, the most blessed and distinguished man Benedict shone forth, as the most brilliant and eloquent author of a cenobitic rule and the most discerning founder of all monastic discipline. Just at that time, the saintly Pope John was presiding over the holy and apostolic see in Rome, who was, according to rumor, slain by the Arian King Theoderic, a most violent persecutor of the orthodox. (That fierce patron of Arian perversity also murdered the patrician Symmachus.) Whoever desires to know everything about the life of this most holy Benedict should read the second book of the

Dialogues of Blessed Gregory. There one will find described in a clear and orderly fashion how Benedict was schooled from his boyhood, and how he converted [to the monastic life]. But there is as well his extraordinary working of miracles, both famous and sublime, which we remember before all else. I have taken from that book only those matters thought suitable to place in this, my own little work; but I also wished to reveal to my readers, into whose hands the other volume might not come, how the disciple of that most excellent master was able to carry out the works of perfection easily, insofar as God assisted him, as the companion of his Master, gaining strength by the prayers and the merits of Benedict's teaching and learning, just as one grows out of the cradle with nourishing milk, as the saying goes.

8. The most blessed Maurus was descended from a most distinguished family of senators; his father was Eutychius and his mother named Julia. When he was twelve years old, his parents entrusted him to the most holy Benedict to be reared in the service of almighty God within a monastic environment. While he was as yet a youth, he grew strong in the monastic virtues, as I myself witnessed; I also frequently observed how he began to serve as the master's assistant (*adjutor*) and then as the co-worker (*cooperator*) of his miracles. The most holy Benedict always loved him more dearly than all others and instructed him, forming him thereby into the service of almighty God as second to none in most sacred observance of the monastery. Who indeed ever more austerely subdued his own body with fasts, abstinence, vigils, rough clothing and great cold? Frequently we observed him during the holy days of Lent wearing neither tunic nor cowl but only a hair shirt; only twice a week would he taste even a very little food, and he never finished a meal. Of course this was the most holy Benedict's own custom throughout his life: inspired by his example, he mortified his flesh severely—to the degree that his father permitted it. During the rest of the year he always wore a very rough hair shirt under his monastic tunic, reaching from his shoulders to his loins while his bed was a heap of pebbles and stones, and for a covering he used only haircloth, except during Lent. Then he tried insofar as he could to sleep, not lying down, but standing up, and if fatigue overcame him, he would steal some sleep sitting down. No one ever saw him rise from his bed with the rest of the brothers; rather he always anticipated the Night

Office with a vigil: He usually recited fifty psalms, often a hundred, and on occasion the entire psalter, before celebrating the night office while during the intervals between the hours, he poured out prayers of sorrow, weeping copiously. He also made time for silence and reading so conscientiously that the most holy Benedict himself found him worthy of admiration.

9. As he grew in virtue, by means of these and other practices it would take too long to describe, the most holy Benedict referred to him in the assembly of all the brothers; suppressing his name as if he were speaking about someone else, he urged the junior monks and the less diligent to follow his lead. 'We have been witnessing', he said, 'in our own day a youth of the most honorable nobility, still in his early years, who is so quick to grasp the entirety of monastic life that he might easily be thought of an age with some of the elders'. Now some of the brothers and the most blessed Maurus himself, most beloved of God, surely knew that Benedict was saying these things about him, but he never fell into the vice of boasting about it. Rather he strove to move with concerted effort from strength to strength, filled with zeal and constantly thirsting for what was more difficult and so more holy.

Chapter two: miracles performed at Monte Cassino

10. In one of the monasteries which Benedict had built, there was a certain monk who could not stand still during prayer. As soon as the monks gave themselves to prayer, he immediately went outside and, with a darkened spirit, meditated on worldly and empty fantasies, busying himself much with vanity and levity through the instigation of a demon, whom he trailed after. Although his abbot had frequently admonished him, he was unwilling to turn away from this empty fantasizing. So he was brought to Abbot Benedict and, although the monk had been severely warned by him, once he had returned to the monastery, he remembered the admonition of the man of God for scarcely two days. On the third day, reverting to his usual custom, he again began wandering about during the time for prayer. When this was reported again to the man of God, he said, 'I will come and correct him myself'. Once he had arrived and the brothers were giving

themselves to their customary prayer, he saw that a small dark figure was dragging the restless monk outside by the hem of his habit. At this point the venerable father said to Maurus, the servant of God, and to Pompeianus, the abbot of that monastery, 'Do you not see what it is pulling that monk outdoors?' They responded, 'No'. He said, 'Let us pray that you too may see what that monk is following'. After he had prayed for two days, Maurus the monk saw it; Pompeianus, however, was not able to see it. Leaving the oratory the next day, the man of God discovered the monk standing outside and struck him with his staff for the blindness of his heart. From that day on the monk endured nothing further from the prompting of the small dark creature, as if the ancient enemy himself had been struck with that blow. Let no one doubt that the holy Maurus participated in this miracle, for his most blessed master chose him to be the witness and partner of such a great sight and display of his power.

11. One day about the same time, while the most holy father Benedict was keeping to his cell, Placid, the son of the patrician Tertullus and a servant of the holy man as well as a monk, had gone out to fetch water from the lake. When he carelessly dropped the vessel he was carrying into the water, he went in after it. Immediately a wave swept him up and carried him off on a course away from the shore. Though seated in his cell, the man of God knew immediately what had happened, and calling his best loved disciple, Maurus, he said to him, 'Brother Maurus, run quickly. The boy who was drawing water from the lake has fallen in, and the wave has already carried him a long way offshore'. A wondrous thing then occurred which has scarcely happened since the time of Peter the Apostle. With a blessing requested and bestowed, Maurus, energized at the command of his father, ran to the place where the wave had carried the boy off; thinking that he was going by land, but was in fact running over the water, he grabbed the boy by his hair and returned, running all the way: As soon as his foot touched the shore, he returned to his senses and, looking back, he realized that he had been running across the water, and what he could not imagine doing had nonetheless, amazingly, come to pass. He then went back and reported the incident to Benedict.

12. The venerable man Benedict attributed this, not to his own merits, but to the obedience of the other. But he, on the contrary, claimed

that it had happened only because of Benedict's command; that he had not been a participant in the miracle because he had been unaware of what he was doing. Then the rescued boy stepped as arbiter into this friendly debate of mutual humility. He said, 'When I was being pulled out of the water, I saw the abbot's sheepskin cloak above my head, so I thought he was pulling me out of the water'. Oh, the admirable holiness of that most blessed man! What he had obtained through holy merits, he decided to attribute to his disciple's obedience, for he knew that Maurus, taught by himself, was capable of working still greater wonders owing to his holy monastic observance, since he had came to understand everything correctly in every detail. However, Charity holds first place in the hearts of the saints and seeks not its own advantage but that of others. So this most worthy Benedict, pleasing to God, had no doubt that the events had occurred through his own merits; he wished, however, to impute them to his holy disciple, so that his [Maurus'] holiness would be recognized by people through the miraculous nature of these signs, whom he [Benedict] had made most beloved of God and most excellent before Him in monastic observance.

13. Likewise, at another time, the excellent father restored an iron sickle that had been given to one of his monks—a Goth—for cutting back some thorn bushes. The sickle had fallen off its handle into the lake. When informed of this by Blessed Maurus, Benedict restored the sickle to the handle from which it had dropped off. Moreover, he once imposed a penance on the disciple I have been discussing above because he had presumed to rejoice in telling Benedict of the death of a certain priest, a persecutor whom Almighty God had struck down in a terrible fashion. Afterwards Benedict gave himself over to deep mourning, either because his enemy was lying in a grave or because his disciple had rejoiced over his death.

14. From these events and others there is much opportunity for demonstrating that, after Maurus had been given over to the tutelage of the holy man, he was either involved in most of his miracles or was his fellow worker (*cooperator*). We know these things most certainly and there can be no doubt about them, above all because once, when Benedict was absent, the Lord willed to work a great miracle through

him in our own monastery. There were as well the many wonders that God willed him to work on the journey—throughout which we were traveling right along with him—and at the monastery where, by God's will, he finally rested.

15. Then one day a certain man, a high nobleman according to worldly ranking, begged the most holy Benedict in person to come to his house and through his merits and prayers to free both his wife and his newborn son from a demon who was afflicting them both terribly. The holy man of God did not delay going as the man was known to him for his good works. The most blessed Maurus—at that time discharging the functions of prior, steward, and administrator of the entire monastery at the holy father's order—had gone out with the brothers rather a long way from the monastery to gather in the crops. As he was returning with the brothers for the noon meal, he encountered on the road, before reaching the gate of the monastery, a boy both dumb and lame. The boy's father and mother threw themselves down at his feet with a great clamor and terrible weeping, begging him in God's name to restore their son to them whole. They entreated him, grasping his knees tightly with their hands, but he shrank from attempting such a miracle, exclaiming that he was a sinner and unable to be the worker of such a miracle: 'Above all', he said, 'because these deeds are the work of the holy Apostles and other perfect men who follow their example by believing and imitating them'. We heard him saying these things, but knowing also that his life and merit were both so excellent and acceptable to God as to be able to work such miracles, we joined together with the parents of the boy in beseeching him to restore the young man from his illness. As a most compassionate man, prostrate in prayer and suffused with tears, after praying at great length, he took from around his neck the stole with which, by order of his blessed master, he had been ordained a deacon that same year. (According to custom and owing to his holiness, he had been wearing the stole constantly during that time.) Making the sign of the cross, he placed the stole on the head of the sick boy and, raising his eyes to heaven, he prayed: 'Lord Jesus Christ, you deigned to make a covenant with your disciples, saying to them, *Amen, I say unto you, believe that everything you ask for in prayer you have received, and it all shall come unto you* [Mark 11:24]. Confirm that promise now insofar as we, your

servants, however insignificant and sinful, have that same faith in you and in your holy words.' Saying these words, he turned to the afflicted boy and said, 'In the name of the holy and undivided Trinity and assisted by the merits of our most holy master, stand up straight, healed and sound'. Restored immediately to health, the boy began to walk about in front of us, perfectly healthy. He blessed God in a voice of rejoicing and praise, saying 'Blessed be God, the Creator of all things, who by the merits of his most holy servant Benedict, through his most blessed disciple Maurus, has willed to restore my health'. When the most excellent Benedict returned to the monastery, with the healings accomplish for which he had gone off, he soon learned what had happened, since we were rehearsing it over and over and praising God. He began henceforth to hold the most blessed Maurus in special admiration and veneration and no longer thought of him as a disciple, seeing that he had been drawn so near to God.

Chapter three: mission to Gaul, departure from Cassino

16. At about the same time, legates came to our monastery from the most blessed Bertigranus, bishop of the city of Le Mans. Having heard of the holiness of our distinguished father, the most holy bishop had sent Flodegard, his archdeacon, and Harderadus, his vicar (*vicedominus*) from his court with great gifts. Both were very admirable men and most vigorous advocates, and they exhorted [Benedict] with many entreaties to send monks perfected in monastic life to build a monastery in the bishop's diocese, where the Rule would be strictly observed. As I set forth in the introduction of this work, our most excellent father knew, both through reason and the revelation of the Holy Spirit, that his end was near. Accordingly he assigned to the episcopal legates the most blessed Maurus and the four of us whose names I mentioned in the preamble. He instructed us that in every matter we should be as totally obedient to the most blessed Maurus, whom he had made our master, as to himself.

17. Who could adequately express how much we mourned? What great lamentation came upon our entire congregation! Ever since our holy father revealed the day of his death, the hope and consolation of

the whole congregation rested on the most blessed Maurus. We had rejoiced that he would rule over us as our father and superior after Benedict's passing. Moved by our tears and sighs, our most holy father spoke as follows, 'Most beloved sons and brothers, so much sadness over such a matter as this! It is surely more fitting for me to mourn than for you, as I am delivering up my greatest support. But, as the apostle says, *Charity is kind*;[1] the kindness of our charity we should then extend in every way towards those whom we know to be greatly in need of it, seeking less our own good than that of others. Therefore I beg you with fatherly love to wipe your tears and temper your mourning. God will grant greater things both to me, after my body has been laid aside, and to this holy community. You have each been brought to holiness far more by the community's merits and example than by my own. I am particularly concerned that no one acquire, through the wiles of the ancient enemy, the power to damage to us by the blight of unhappiness. The vastness of the entire earth cannot separate us, whom the peace of unity has joined together in holy charity; so I shall live on in the form of the interior man, who is made new according to his image who created him, until that time we look upon each other again. And you, most beloved brothers, whom we send to those regions to work the Lord's purpose, act manfully. May your hearts be comforted by the holy Rule and by monastic observance. Be assured beyond any doubt that, however great the austerities you endure for the sake of the salvation of others in this world, so much the greater will be the joy of your God-given eternal rewards. Nor should the dissolution of my miserable body cause you any grief. For I will be even more present to you once the heaviness of the body has been laid aside and, by God's grace, I will be your diligent fellow worker (*cooperator*)'.

18. Having said all this, he embraced us and led us out, along with the entire congregation to the gate of the monastery. Embracing us once more and giving us his blessing, he gave to the most holy Maurus his disciple a copy of the Rule written by his own most holy hand. He then ordered that the balance for [weighing] the pound of bread be brought forth and the bronze vessel containing the measure for the wine. He turned them over with orders not to alter them. To the

1. Cf. 1 Cor 13:4.

bishop, by means of the legates, he then sent an order that he should accept us with fatherly love and, as he had promised, deliver to us a fitting place for the construction of a monastery.

19. We began the journey on the fifth Saturday of Epiphany,[2] stopping first at one of our monastery's possessions, a villa called Euchaeia. There we were received with fitting ceremony by two of our brothers, Probus and Aquinus, whom our holy father had sent one day ahead for this purpose. That night, while we were celebrating the Nocturnal Offices, two more brothers arrived: Honoratus, of happy memory, and Felicissimus, a youth of excellent character and the most holy Maurus' cousin, sent by our most holy father, Benedict. And when we saw them we were overcome with joy, for surely they carried something of great import from our father that we should listen to and learn from. Nor were we mistaken in our judgment. When the morning office hymns had been completed, we gathered together and the monk Honoratus brought forth from his breast a magnificent gift for the blessed Maurus. It was an ivory receptacle for relics, along with a little page of writing. The latter contained few words, but they were laden with the charity of prophetic utterance and of holy affection. The most holy Benedict himself had ordered them to be carried to us quickly before we left the place. Into the reliquary he had placed three fragments from the wood of the life-saving Cross, and relics of the holy Mother of God, of the holy archangel Michael, from the small red altar cloth of his sacred memorial, and of Saint Stephen, the first martyr, and of the blessed confessor of Christ, Martin.

20. The text of the letter, which Blessed Maurus later ordered to be buried with him out of love for his father, contained these words, 'Accept, my most dearly beloved, these last gifts of your teacher. They bear witness to my long-lasting love and may supply you and your comrades with a permanent defense against all the obstructions of evil men. After three times twenty years have been completed, you will have attained monastic perfection and will be introduced to the joy of your Lord. This the Lord yesterday deigned to reveal to me after you

2. That is, on Septuagesima Sunday, the beginning of the pre-Lenten penitential season.

had departed. I also prophesy to you that a time of delay will lengthen your quest, and you will find a suitable place only with difficulty, which events will occur by God's command, while the enemy of humankind will create problems for you by his cunning. Yet the goodness of God's mercy will never fail you: In a manner different from, but superior to, that I had expected, He will for some time put your hearts' desire to the test, but then his goodness will bestow on you a suitable dwelling place. Now, have courage! As you are happy in departing so you will be even happier in your arrival.' When these words had been read out, Blessed Maurus became cheerful about the mission he had been found worthy to undertake, but about which he had also been warned. So he sent back his brothers to Benedict's presence with gratitude; he also repeatedly impressed upon his cousin Felicissimus the need for a more perfect religious observance.

Chapter four: miracles of Vercelli and Aguane

21. Proceeding on our way, we arrived at Vercelli on the fifty-fifth day of our journey. There we were hosted by two clerics of the city, who received us with the fullest measure of charity. It was here also that the prophecy of our holy father already began to be fulfilled. Harderadus, whom I mentioned, was climbing the steps of a very lofty and impressive tower when he fell down headlong, the Devil blocking his way. His whole body was so smashed that he was actually wrapped in a shroud and carried, practically dead, to our lodging. We all despaired of his life. This accident caused the deepest sorrow, especially to the archdeacon Flodegard. We were delayed for two weeks while the victim was continually weakened by his deepening and intractable pain. His right hand and arm, up to his shoulder, had become so inflamed that we anxiously searched for a doctor to amputate it.

22. At dawn of the thirteenth day after we arrived, Flodegard exclaimed that he could not bear that it be amputated. He burst into the oratory where Blessed Maurus was taking some leisure for prayer; embracing his legs and covering them with his tears, he begged the most holy man to help the sick cleric by his prayers and power. He pleaded with him not to allow the suffering of the amputating knife and the

burning to torment his companion, for he knew that [Maurus] could easily restore him to health by his intervention. Blessed Maurus was indeed moved to tears both by the misery of the injured man and by the flood of the cleric's imploring tears—and by this delay in the journey. Therefore he placed himself before the altar in protracted prayers of petition, beating on the ears of heaven with sighs and weeping; then from the altar—before which he had thrown himself down prostrate in the form of a cross—he retrieved the reliquary which his most blessed Master had sent to him, and handing it to us, he went to the bed of the sufferer. Renewing his prayers, he uncovered the life-giving wood and with it made a sign of the cross that extended from the sick man's shoulder to the end of his hand. Then he prayed aloud, 'Oh Lord, maker of all creatures, who for the restoration of the human race caused your only begotten Son, by the working of the Holy Spirit, to be made flesh out of the ever-virgin Mary, who graciously willed to come to our aid, delivering us from the wounds and weaknesses of our souls through the most holy and glorious wood of the life-giving cross, so through the power of this wood of life, be pleased to restore his man to his original health'. As soon as Blessed Maurus had ended these petitions, all the warmth of the blood immediately began to course through the three areas where the whole arm had swelled. This was that same Harderadus, a nobleman according to the ranking of the world, yet more worthy in his religious zeal—insofar as this was possible for a secular person.

23. Flodegard, having witnessed such a miracle, was unable to hold back his tears of joy. He glorified God and continuously extolled our most holy father Benedict as worthy of possessing and training such disciples through whom God carried out such wonders. The whole suburban population also crowded around, each person hoping to be blessed by seeing or touching blessed Maurus. But he fled from the sight of the crowd that sought him, avid not for his own glory but always for the glory of his Father who is in heaven. He said, 'Though no one can doubt that this cure was obtained by the merits of our most holy father, Benedict, it should instead be ascribed, not to a man, but to the great Redeemer of all, who was pleased to work this miracle through the wood of our salvation'. Our invalid, meanwhile, just newly out of danger, implored Maurus not to leave the city on the fol-

lowing day until he was able fittingly to return thanks to God for what he had been given. He wished to offer praise and the sacrifice of true confession through all the houses of prayer that had been built there. Maurus willingly assented to this petition, because he greatly loved him, seeing that Harderadus favored the zeal of our Order.

24. We finally left the city on the fifteenth day and tried to quicken the pace of our assigned journey. But while we were crossing the ridges of the Alps close to midday, our servant Sergius fell off the horse he was riding onto a huge rock on the left. When he tried to get up, he twisted his foot so badly that all the bones were crushed together. They no longer looked like parts of a foot but like some single smooth object. He seemed at some moments to stop breathing, and the most blessed Maurus, greatly affected by so much suffering, came up to the servant and, taking his crushed foot in his left hand, made the sign of the cross over him with his other hand, saying, 'In the name of almighty God, who by his power released those in bonds, stand up healed. Continue your service to the servants of God to which our most blessed father assigned you'. He was made completely whole at that moment, which stirred up immeasurable joy among us.

25. Then, thanks to our prayers, we all arrived at the church of the precious martyr of Christ, Maurice and his companions. There a certain man, blind from his mother's womb, sat outside the basilica daily, begging food from those going in and out. He discovered from the companions of our journey that Maurus, the disciple of the most holy Benedict—the fame of whose holiness had now become widely known—had arrived at that place. As we were coming out of the entrance to the basilica after prayer, this same blind man stretched his whole body out full on the ground, imploring as follows, 'I entreat you, Maurus, servant of God, by these precious martyrs of the Theban legion, in the name of your venerable master Benedict, that by your own prayers the Lord may be pleased to grant sight to my eyes'. When he heard this, the most holy man of God stood still for a few moments on the step and instructed the blind man to rise from the pavement. As he was standing before him, he asked, 'Tell me, how much time has passed while you have been here at the sacred gates of the holy martyrs?' To which he responded, 'Almost eleven years have now gone

by.' The holy man of the Lord responded, 'These holy martyrs, dear to God, exposed their sacred bodies to be slain by gladiators for the sake of Christ that they might place their souls before him. If they desired that the Lord give sight to your eyes, could they not have accomplished that? Take heed then to beseech them in prayer. Their deeds are greater than ours, and we are no less in need of their intercession than the rest of humankind.' Having said this, he began to move away, but the blind man would not stop shouting loud and fearsome oaths until at our urging, the holy man pressed the fingers of his right hand on the blind man's tear-soaked eyes, into which the splendor of the sun had never yet shown. Gazing towards heaven for a long time, he then he made the sign of our redemption over the blind man's eyes and prayed, 'May our Lord and Saviour Jesus Christ, who is the true light, enlightening every person who comes into this world, be pleased to heal your blindness through this invocation of his holy name and the merits of these, your blessed saints, and of our master Benedict. As you come to perceive the wonderful works of the Most High with which he has pleased to adorn his earthly creation, may you praise the Creator of all and our Redeemer with exaltation.'

26. As soon as the holy man had prayed this, the blood began to course abundantly throughout the blind man's eyes. Gazing about at the sphere of the sun and its bright rays, he began in a ringing voice to chant the Canticle of the Three Children[3] verse by verse. The man's name was Linus, as he later informed us. He had learned both the psalter and the day and night offices by hearing them constantly. When they saw the miracle worked through Blessed Maurus, the inhabitants of the town came together in a throng, begging him to impart his blessing to them, and he agreed, 'May the Lord our God, who dwells in Sion, bless you that you may see his good things which are in Jerusalem all the days of your life', and he gave an order to the former blind man: He should never depart from that church but should continually serve the Lord and the holy martyrs there. The man faithfully carried out this commandment. After the passing of blessed Maurus, as we were returning to our monastery, we discovered him in the same church performing

3. Dan 3:47-88.

the duties of the clerical state, though he was by then experiencing a feeble old age.

Chapter Five: The Visit to Saint Romanus and the Death of Benedict

27. From there we set out again, traveling more quickly on our appointed journey. One night we lodged in Jura, next to the church of the most holy mother of God and ever-virgin Mary. A widow named Remeia lived in the house next to us with her son, a young boy whom she had been raising since the recent death of her husband. He was dying, lying on his bed and drawing his last breath, while she spent a sleepless night lamenting and wailing. As was his custom, the man of God Maurus went into the church while we were sleeping to render his prayers and supplications to God. Yet when the time for the morning office approached, and the woman had not for a moment ceased from her weeping and moaning, the man of God, tenderly moved to pity for her, prostrated himself before God with tears and prayed that He would deign to have mercy on the wretched woman by safely restoring her son to her safe and sound. When he had risen from prayer, he came secretly into the cell where we were sleeping. He gently shook the monk Simplicius, making a sign that he should follow quietly. Having followed him into the church he waited, bewildered at what he might be ordered to do. Coming up to him the Lord's holy man said, 'My soul has deep pity on the sorrows of this unlucky woman. So let us, filled with faith, go over together to the bed where he is lying; perhaps grace from above will restore him'.

28. Coming with Simplicius to the pallet of the boy's now almost dead body, he said: 'Christ our Lord and Saviour, the single hope and consolation of those who suffer and persevere, was moved to have pity on the widow whose son who had been carried outside the gates, and raised him up amidst a crowd of onlookers, now, by that same pity, have mercy on this woman by restoring her son safe and sound'. He said this and then departed. The young man, who now had lain for two days silent and unconscious, called out to his mother, saying, 'Mother, do not weep, for by the tears of that servant of God, which

he poured out in pity for your sorrow, I have been returned from the jaws of hell to life and health'. His mother said to him, 'Look! He is in our basilica, singing morning hymns as usual with his companions'; the young man as if not at all indisposed, rising immediately from his bed, went out, entered the church and without hesitation approached the most holy Maurus, crying aloud and saying, 'Truly you are the one who by your tears and merits brought me back to the upper world, whence I escaped the dolorous sentence of the tribunal which had condemned me to the infernal places'. The report of this deed immediately ran through the entire region. Men and women alike ran down the road headlong towards us, and on all sides old men with children together sang praises to God, who so exalts his holy ones.[4] That young man's name was Alagoas, who, we later learned, became a monk in the monastery of Lérins.

29. Because the Easter solemnity was close at hand, we hastened on our way more quickly every day. On the day when the Lord's Last Supper is celebrated, we arrived at the neighborhood of Auxerre. Blessed Maurus, hearing a report that the monk Romanus, the assistant (*coadjutor*) and co-worker (*cooperator*) of our most blessed father Benedict at the outset of his monastic life—as is set out at length in the history of his life—had made for Gaul following a revelation, and had built a small monastery in the district, at a place called Font-Rouge. Asking the guides of our expedition to turn aside so that we might celebrate the holy Pasch there, Blessed Maurus made for the site, mostly because he knew that on the following day our most holy Master would pass on; he also looked forward to enjoying a conversation with Blessed Romanus. The guides of our journey freely acceded to the request of the man of God and hurried at a quick pace to reach the monastery.

30. We arrived at the sixth hour on Good Friday and were received by Blessed Romanus. Those of us who had traveled with Blessed Maurus were put to work setting in order everything that was needed for the feast day, while the two exceedingly holy men held sweet converse with each other on the life eternal. Evening was falling after the solemn office, which is every year specially celebrated, when holy

4. Cf. Ps 148:12.

Maurus, the man of God, said to Blessed Romanus, 'Tomorrow, our most blessed father Benedict, having cast off the weight of his earthly body, will ascend to his heavenly home, happy and rejoicing'. On hearing this, Saint Romanus began weeping inconsolably, dissolving in tears. Hoping to console him, Blessed Maurus said, 'We ought to rejoice, not to weep this way at his passing, because we are sending on ahead of us a mighty patron. He will be more present to us now than if he lived on in the flesh'. Despite these words, however, he could not hold back his own tears. On that night, the twelfth of the kalends of April [March 20th] as the most sacred vigil of Easter approached, the most blessed Maurus—and we who had come with him, along with Saint Romanus and all his disciples—fasted and kept the vigil and, as was the custom at that time in the Roman Church, we each recited the psalms silently to ourselves and sent forth prayerful petitions for the passing of our father Benedict, God's best beloved.

31. As the third hour of that holy day came to an end, the most blessed Maurus remained in the church, so that even from afar off he might, by suitable prayer and psalmody, help to make Benedict's passing safe, at whatever hour it should happen. Suddenly, he was taken up in the spirit, and saw himself transported back to the place whence we had come. There he beheld a road strewn with rich coverings and gleaming with innumerable torches. It stretched away from Benedict's cell towards heaven on a straight easterly course. Two brothers of our congregation were his companions in the vision, with whom at the very same moment, he gazed at the identical vision. As they marveled greatly at the road they were gazing at, a shining figure of venerable aspect from above appeared, standing nearby, asked them whose path it was that they were looking upon. To whom they responded that they did not know; so he said to them, 'This is the way by which Benedict, the beloved of God, ascended to heaven'. One of the two brothers who saw this vision along with Blessed Maurus was living in our monastery, but the other, as Blessed Gregory writes, saw it from far off.[5] Soon after this, came to himself and immediately called Saint Romanus and ourselves together. He told us everything which he had seen, just as it had occurred.

5. *Dialogues* II.37.

32. We then completed the celebrations of that solemn day and the Sunday following, when the triumph of the Lord's Resurrection is venerated with special rejoicing. On the second day of that feast, before we set out, Saint Romanus said to Blessed Maurus, 'If, without danger to my soul, I could leave this place, I would far rather abide with you, most beloved brother, than end my life in any other place. But because it is perilous to leave these regions and because my last days are at hand, go forth with a blessing to where you have been sent; may your fortunes prosper. May almighty God be always with you and with the brothers who journey with you, and may he lead you by a straight path towards the true land of promise which he has been pleased to set before all his chosen ones. He has prepared for them there what neither eye has seen nor ear heard, nor has it entered into the heart of man, the heart of those who, having set aside all worldly things and given themselves up to heavenly desires, may say with the apostle, "But God has given us the revelation of these things through his Spirit."'[6]

Chapter six: arrival at Anjou

33. Leaving that place we soon came to the road into Orléans. At that point a heavy sadness entered into our guides. They heard by certain messengers that the blessed Bertigranus [bishop of Le Mans] had gone to the Lord, and another bishop had already been set in his place. When they informed Blessed Maurus and us of this, we began to sink into depression, not knowing what we should do. But Blessed Maurus remembered our most holy Father's prophecy: He had foretold that we would be brought to a suitable place, though with difficulty. So he rallied our dejected spirits with soothing consolations, promising us, 'Most beloved brothers, do not let your spirits sink because of the sadness of our present straits: God is accustomed to overcoming the troubles of those who suffer and raises them up by his grace. The prayers of our most blessed father will also assist us, who promised always to be present as our fellow worker (*cooperator*). The patriarch Abraham left his house and his relatives by God's command and after-

6. 1 Cor 2:9-10.

wards received the land of his pilgrimage as an inheritance. Just so, rejoicing to have undertaken our own pilgrimage, we, as truly devoted servants, expect consolation from the Lord as we try, through it all, to follow the footsteps of our most holy father Benedict. He left forever his house and the possessions of his homeland and finally ran away secretly from his own nurse, longing to please God alone by every means. He thereby amply deserved such great grace from God that he was second to none after the first and most blessed Apostles; indeed, by God's help, he became the founder of such holy monasteries that he gained for God thousands of most excellent monks.

34. This exhortation of Blessed Maurus comforted us exceedingly and we began to discuss with our guides about how we might best proceed. The high nobleman Harderadus sat down beside Blessed Maurus and began suggesting the following: 'It seems to me to be worthy and proper, holy father and devout brothers, that we who discharged this legation by order of our bishop, for the sake of which we have passed through such vast expanses of land, should now approach this new and unknown bishop. We can make the purpose of our journey known to him in detail and thereby ascertain his will regarding this mission. At the same time we will have the opportunity to carry our own views to him. But you, venerable father, along with the brothers you have with you, should expect us to return here—I should say, within a week. Even if he declines to do what his blessed predecessor had intended, some other way will surely be found, by divine assistance, to accomplish what you have been sent to do. You will not have taken such a laborious journey for nothing.' Having said this, they then lodged us in a most suitable house in the same city next to the church of Blessed Peter the Apostle. They assigned to care for us the most honorable persons in their own service, instructing them at the same time to take no less care in their obligations towards Blessed Maurus and ourselves as to the others. When all this had been graciously arranged, they set out with the holy Maurus' blessing.

35. When they arrived at Le Mans and were announced to the bishop, they were received by him honorably. He reinstated them in their offices and indeed augmented the perquisites of their former positions. Then when they explained to him the reason for their legation and

asked what he wished to do regarding the mission, the bishop responded that he wished to pursue the projects which he had himself begun rather than those of others, lest he seem to be building upon another's foundation. 'Especially', he added, 'since the orderly administration of my own affairs and the vigilant oversight of the churches lies heavy on me'. Now this happened according to the hidden counsel of God, who had chosen the place that would be raised up by the teaching of Blessed Maurus and the establishment of the discipline of the Rule. It was his will that this should not be delayed by any pretext or by an inappropriate site. In fact, the place which had been set aside for the building of the monastery by the most blessed Bertigranus was neither appropriate nor well-suited to the observance of the Rule, as our guides reported to us. Indeed from the name itself, Rupiacus [Rocky], we thought it must be a rough and rocky place.

36. Harderadus, understanding very clearly that Bishop Duomnolus was unwilling to do anything about this matter, became elated and asked leave to return to us. When that had been granted, he sent his nephew, Hademarus, a vigorous youthful fellow, to Blessed Maurus, to encourage him to avoid a drooping spirit, but, as quickly as he could, to hasten with all his companions to a place in Anjou where he would meet us, as the messenger would designate. Both Blessed Maurus and all of us who had stayed with him were much excited by such news, so on the tenth day after we had entered the town of Orléans, we departed, hurrying to the designated meeting place.

37. After five days we came to a place called Restis, where we met the honorable Harderadus and his wife and sons, who had already been waiting there for us for two days. When they had received us honorably and prepared refreshments, Harderadus took his wife, named Caecilia, and Blessed Maurus somewhat aside and told him everything he had learned from the bishop. Blessed Maurus said to him, 'What should we do now, most noble sir, or rather, what do you think would be best?' As he was a man of a most agreeable countenance, Harderadus answered amiably, 'My nephew, whose name is Florus, is a man powerful in possessions, both here and in other regions. As the first among the great magnates of the kingdom of the Franks, he most fittingly directs all official business he is instructed to undertake by the palace. Though he

has been thus established in such worldly power, from his youth he has taken great care to please almighty God. He sent away his wife, whom he had been forced to marry owing to pressure from the king and our families. From that union he had a single son. If he could somewhere find men perfected in monastic discipline, he would build a monastery on his own land, which came to him through a paternal inheritance, and he longs to offer his son to God there, as well. Moreover, once he has left all the business of this world behind and is free of it all, he himself longs to serve God in that same monastery. Therefore I will send to him my messenger, who can explain why you have come and can ascertain whether he is still of the same mind. Meanwhile, until he himself or the messenger returns, if it pleases you, let us look over the place of which I have been speaking.

Chapter seven: the foundation of the monastery of Glanfeuil

38. Hearing this, Blessed Maurus was exceedingly joyful and on the next day went with the nobleman to examine the location. Now at that time, Theudebert, king of the realm of the Franks, was nobly governing as supreme ruler. The most excellent Florus, introduced above, was his intimate, so dear to the king in everything that he obtained permission from him to do anything he might want in all his domain, and no one objected. When Harderadus' envoy brought him the news of our arrival and the bishop of Le Mans' refusal to receive us, he immediately went to the king and explained the reason for our coming. He then informed the king of his desire to construct a monastery and asked his permission to allow us to build his long-desired abbey. Theudebert responded, 'You have always served me so well that I can deny you nothing—or even argue with you. Therefore, as our companion by our favor and strengthened by our authority, receive these very holy men with all reverence. Carry out with them the desire which the grace from above has placed within you. Appeal to them, too, to implore mercy for us, our children, and the entire people of the kingdom that God has conferred upon us. They will find us very well prepared and most prompt to render every service, if we find that they indeed manifest the sort of monastic observance that by common

report their master Benedict so carefully passed on to them. It will be your responsibility to gather together artisans from wherever in our realm you can find them, so that the task can be completed quickly. The realm will provide all the resources needed to construct the project suitably, according to your will and counsel'.

39. Encouraged by the king's numerous and generous promises, the most noble Florus arrived quickly at the estate he possessed called Glanfeuil. Hearing of his arrival, Harderadus and Blessed Maurus met him at the entrance to the gates. When Florus saw Blessed Maurus standing by, dressed in a very modest monastic tunic, he immediately leapt from his horse, approached him and three times stretched out his entire body upon the earth and when he had been humbly and modestly received, [Maurus] raised him up, as he had learned to do and for several moments they delayed, restraining each other, embracing, each suffused with tears of joy. After embracing us all, the nobleman took Blessed Maurus by his right hand, and again briefly enfolding him, said, 'We rejoice that you have come, servant of the high God and disciple of the most holy man Benedict, whose name and renown, deservedly won through his service to God, has become known to almost every time and place. We bless as well the glorious name of the Lord who sent you and your companions, those revered men, to help us in this province.' After saying this, Florus led him to the house, with Harderadus and his son preceding them.

40. On the next day, after the morning office, we came together and Blessed Maurus revealed his intention to build a monastery, at the same time reminding us of the promises of the king and his request for fervent prayers on behalf of himself, his sons, and of all his people. Continuing this line of thought, Blessed Maurus said to Florus, 'The observances of our order demand the greatest quiet and security. Therefore if it does not appear contrary to the munificence of your generosity, we should first of all pass through and examine carefully the property which, as you declare, you wish to hand over to God and his servants for the salvation of your soul. Once a deed is drawn up and you hand it over in the presence of witnesses, we can then legally receive the property into our seigniorial possession. To which Florus proffered his agreement; three days later, they returned to the estate, after inspecting the entire property on horseback.

41. Then, following the advice of the most blessed man, the most excellent Florus conveyed all the property to him by written deed, transferring it out of his own jurisdiction to the authority and seigniorial lordship of the other. On that same day, he offered his son, Bertulf, to the Lord. A young boy of about eight, he was to be brought up and instructed in our monastic discipline under the tutelage and authority of the most blessed Maurus, just as he himself had been educated by his most holy master Benedict. After the oblation of the young man, Florus spoke further to Blessed Maurus, 'It is only fitting, most holy one, that you and your companions be secure not only in respect to this place but to the other goods that I wish to bestow on you. Now that I have offered my son to the service of God under your tutelage, I promise, God willing, that having completed my own life as count and with my duty done, I will leave behind everything that is of the world and bind myself to the service of God in this same place.'

42. Once workers and artisans had been assembled and the foundations laid, the work went forward quickly day after day. The area was small, sloping downward above the riverbank. On one end the hill was an obstacle, while on the other the bank of the Loire hemmed it in; so they began building the monastery on the lower slope of the hill. First a large house of prayer was constructed, which Blessed Maurus ordered consecrated in honor of Saint Martin the confessor of Christ. The most holy Benedict had placed an altar of the most blessed Martin in his own oratory after demolishing the altar of Apollo, and ordered that he be buried there. Following his example, his most excellent disciple ordered that his own body be laid to rest in an oratory of the same dedication. Since the above-mentioned Florus had obtained from King Theudebert final authority in the entire realm and was also acting as viscount in the territory of Anjou, he had been able to collect the most skilled craftsmen, men experienced in woodworking, stonemasons and others well versed in the other crafts.

43. One day, while he was inspecting the workmen with Blessed Maurus, he sat down with the man of God, who was reading as he rested and now and then explained to Florus what he was studying. Now Florus had brought from the king's own palace a certain cleric who was overseeing the stone cutting. He fell over backwards from the

topmost steps on which the workmen were standing as they built the wall upwards and struck a heap of rocks that were being carried away. Although everyone thought he was dead—since the blood was pouring out of every orifice—and they talked of nothing except where to bury him, the man of God came up with Florus and immediately had the victim carried off to the entranceway of the church of Blessed Martin. Once everyone had left, he gave himself to prayer, prostrate before the altar. Completing his prayer, he went outside again and made the sign of the cross over the man's crushed limbs, praying, 'In His name who formed the body of man from the slime of the earth and breathed into him the breath of life: 'Arise, Langisus, be healed and finish the task you have begun.' The man immediately revived, as if rising from sleep, and wondered how he had arrived at that place. God's holy one said to him, 'You didn't come here on your own two feet; you were carried by the hands of others. But be off as quick as you can, so that the work is not interrupted by your absence.' After the man had gone off, Florus, who had been standing on one side with the monk Simplicius, observed all that the man of God had done. Florus ran over to him and threw himself at his feet, crying out, 'Holy Maurus, you are truly the disciple of blessed Benedict, of whom we have often heard such great things'. From that day on, Florus held him in the greatest reverence and dared not approach too closely.

44. When the cleric who had been healed had returned to his work, some of the laborers began to slander Blessed Maurus, claiming he had left his monastery and come to this remote land not for religious reasons but out of greed, for which he had been rather well-known in other regions. They said that his deeds were accomplished not through the power of God, but through evil spells. As they chattered about this among themselves, an evil spirit suddenly entered into three of them and began to batter them with attacks so dreadful that the very life was ripped out of one of them, a man named Flodegisus. The man of God recognized what had happened and began to weep copiously. Again he entered the oratory of Blessed Martin and prayed fervently, both for those who were still tormented and for the man who had died. After he had spent three hours in uninterrupted prayer, he approached those who were tormented and were now biting each other. Three times he made the sign of the cross over them and prayed, 'The only-begotten

Son of God, our Lord Jesus Christ, gave to his disciples the power of trampling upon the serpents and scorpions of the earth and over all the powers of the enemy. May he free you from this diabolic torture.' The laborers, however, went on gnashing their teeth and covered themselves with dirt, so the man of God moved closer and placed the fingers of each hand in their mouths. Thereupon the unclean spirits fled through their victims' excrement, leaving stinking traces behind them.

45. Then the man of the Lord ordered the body of the dead man to be lifted up and carried off to the entrance of the church. He passed the entire night in watching, beseeching the Lord constantly with groaning, asking that he deign to restore the soul of the dead man to his body, lest the demon who snatched his soul away should triumph. At first light, he admitted Simplicius the priest, and ordered that the sacrifice of our redemption be offered to God for the worker's soul. After Mass had been completed very devoutly, the man of God approached with Simplicius the place where the dead man lay. He then prayed, 'Lord Jesus Christ, who raised Lazarus from the dead after four days and who at the petition of your servant Elijah restored the son of the widow to life,[7] be now with us, your servants. Restore to the body of this dead man the soul which by your leave, has departed from it owing to the tortures of the enemy of the human race.' As soon as he had said this, the body of the dead man was violently shaken, and he straightaway stood up alive and accepted the command of Maurus that, if he wished to live, he should never again come into the area, however many years he might enjoy. The holy man commanded this solely out of humility, lest he should appear to seek people's applause for the miracle he had worked.

Chapter Eight: The Donations of King Theudebert. The Entry of Florus into Monastic Life

46. By the eighth year after we had arrived, the construction of all the monastery's buildings was fittingly completed and was dedicated by the bishop of the diocese, the most holy Eutropius, who ruled the church of Angers at the time. Four churches had been constructed

7. Jn 11:38-44 and I Kgs 17:23.

within the monastery itself: The largest of these, in which the brothers gathered for the daily offices, was consecrated in honor of Blessed Peter, prince of the apostles; the second, as was noted earlier in honor of Blessed Martin; and the third, smaller than the others, in veneration of Saint Severinus; and the fourth, which was constructed in the form of a lofty four-sided tower at the entrance of the monastery, was dedicated to the holy Archangel Michael.

47. When all this had been completed, Florus, mindful of his promise to God, approached King Theudebert. He asked leave of the king to take up the monastic habit and to redeem, through fasting and prayers and other meritorious works, the many sins he had committed through his activities in the world. Although the king could not deny his request, however unhappy he was to be separated from him, he granted his wish, but kept him for some days at the palace. He questioned him closely regarding the miracles that had been worked through Blessed Maurus, about the strictness of the monastic life he observed with his brothers, and about the number of monks who had now gathered there. When Florus had told him what he knew of a certainty about these matters, the king said to him, 'If I knew it would be pleasing to this servant of God, I would very much like to visit him and see the monastery and to honor him with my royal gift.' To him Florus responded, 'May it please Your Highness, we should seek first to discover the will of the man of God about this visit. You could then satisfy your own desires in accord with his wishes.'

48. After delaying him for some time in his embrace, the king sent Florus on his way, instructing him as follows, 'Be sure to send word back to us quickly after you have met with the holy man at his monastery. If at all possible, I wish to be present on the day that you receive the tonsure'. Coming to the monastery, accompanied by many of the best and noble men from the royal palace, Florus accordingly made known the king's will to the man of God. After he had replied that, so far as he could see, nothing stood in the way of a visit, indeed that he would be most welcome, he ordered Florus to fix a day on which the king should come to the monastery. When he duly arrived in the splendor befitting his royal dignity, he was received by Blessed Maurus and his congregation, a most holy flock whose number now exceeded forty.

After praying among the brothers, the king, clad in royal purple—little regarding his royal dignity—humbly prostrated himself and, weeping copiously, implored Blessed Maurus and the congregation to petition the Lord on his behalf. When the man of God raised him up from the floor, the king said to him, 'We have long been aware of the reputation of your master Benedict. We now rejoice greatly that his renowned deeds of holiness and power are daily continued through you.'

49. The king then requested of Blessed Maurus that the brothers receive him into their prayer fellowship (*societas*) and write his name among theirs. He specially entrusted his son Theudebald to the holy man and to the brothers, advising him to be always devoted to the congregation and in all matters to act as its helper (*adjutor*) and defender. He then inquired of the man of God which brothers had come with him. He pointed us out, asking us to stand apart from the others. The king gazed upon us attentively and asked each of us our name. When he had learned these, he embraced us and then the rest of the community. Seeing Bertulf standing among the rest of the brothers, he asked who he might be. When Blessed Maurus indicated that he was the son of Florus, the king called him over and pressed him to his breast. He then went on to commend him especially to Blessed Maurus out of his great love for the boy's father and asked that he be brought up and educated most lovingly.

50. The king then made a circuit around the monastery, examining it and praising it all as fittingly constructed. He reentered the church of Saint Peter and at that point bestowed on the monastery a royal fisc called LeBois, with all its estates and revenues, that he himself held. He summoned Ansebaldus, who was in charge of the copyists of royal deeds, and ordered that a deed be drawn up for these properties before he quit the monastery so he might confirm it with the royal signet, as was customary. He also granted to Blessed Maurus free access to the king, wherever he might be, if he wished to approach him with any request. Finally [the king] placed a valuable covering on the altar of Saint Peter, along with a golden cross adorned with very precious stones.

51. Going up to the king, Florus then requested the king to order written down as a royal edict to be made before a witness the goods

from his own possessions that he was transferring to the monastery. The king very willingly agreed. After this, in the presence of the king, this same count offered to the Lord and his saints on this special day gifts in profusion, fashioned of gold and silver and precious stones, and a multiplicity of vestments. He freed twenty of his servants as well, first enriching them with great gifts. Finally, he approached the most holy altar, with Blessed Maurus and the entire congregation standing to one side and the king along with a large crowd of attendants on the other, and placed upon the altar his knight's buckler, which he had so often made use of. At the man of God's order, the king, immediately after him, cut off some of the hair from his [Count Florus'] head, followed by any of his nobles who wished to participate. The king shed tears of joy at the devotion of this soul. He then summoned Florus' nephew, Landramnus, and bestowed on him, by means of the royal scepter which he held in his hand, whatever his uncle Florus had held by royal grant.

52. The Lord's holy one requested the king to favor them by entering an elegant and well appointed building most suitably constructed for the reception of guests. As soon as the king had entered, the man of God prostrated himself before the king's feet.[8] The king raised him up, much concerned, and asked what he required. He replied, 'This is my request on behalf of all the servants of God who dwell in this monastery: that the king may come with his servants and with our gratitude partake of the food and drink which the humble labor of the monks has prepared out of devotion.' The king tried to refuse and excuse himself, but one of his councilors, a wise man named Ebbo, said to him, 'My Lord King, you should consider who has issued this invitation to refresh yourself. As Your Highness has observed, these men are the servants of God, and if you disappoint them by refusing, you will not enjoy God's favor.' After hearing this, the king immediately agreed to enter.

53. Before he and his company took their leave—fully refreshed with the monastery's offering of food—[King Theudebert] ordered his well-beloved servant Florus to be brought before him. He was led in dressed in the monastic habit, and the king, moved to tears, said to him, 'I give thanks to almighty God for your monastic vocation! Now you must

8. Cf. RB 53.6-7.

take care and be vigilant that, just as when you dressed in worldly garb, you lived ever nobly with vigor and honor, so now you may progress daily ever higher in this holy monastic life. Strive always to please God without fault until you are able to behold in happy blessedness the God of gods in Zion.' After concluding this admonition, he lingered for some time with Florus. Then, strengthened by the blessing he had requested of Blessed Maurus, he returned to Anjou that same day.

Chapter nine: the death of Florus. Donations of kings Theodebald and Chlothar

54. The next day, Blessed Maurus went out to inspect and formally receive the royal fisc that the king had given to the monastery. After he had been there two days, there was brought before him a paralytic who had lain on his bed at the estate for seven years, having lost all feeling in his body. When the man of God had blessed him, he was restored to perfect health, as if he had never suffered from that miserable affliction.

55. Once back at the monastery, he carefully examined the life and habits of each of those living there, as his own master had done, conveying the word of life to them all, both publicly and in private. Exposing the manifold crafty snares of the ancient enemy, he exhorted them to progress daily to better deeds. Ever since the second year of our arrival, noblemen had gathered there from all over, wishing to devote themselves to the service of almighty God and to follow the holy man's communal life, and not a few offered their sons to God to be brought up under his tutelage. So it was that by the twenty-sixth year after the foundation of the monastery, the community had brought together one hundred and forty brothers. Blessed Maurus wrote this number down and it was settled by his authority and that of the community that this limit should never be exceeded or reduced. The resources of their properties sufficed for the necessities of that number of brothers; if it were exceeded, suffering and want could result.

56. But to return to the subject from which I have digressed: For twelve years, three months and as many days, the aforesaid most noble

Florus—as became his noble rank and character—had observed the monastic regime with perfect holiness. On the twelfth of the calends of September[9] he spent his final day, happily going to the Lord. Meanwhile his son Bertulf was achieving excellence in every holy observance, as a following section will demonstrate.

57. King Theudebert, after he had governed the kingdom of the Franks nobly and vigorously for fourteen years, left the throne to his son Theudebald. This king greatly loved both Blessed Maurus and our community as long as he lived, in accord with the solemn command of his father. He followed in the footsteps of his father, who had nobly honored the monastery of this community whenever he visited us, as I have set forth in detail above. After the death of his father, whenever King Theudebald visited Blessed Maurus and the monastery, he was no less generous as befit his regal magnificence. So he conferred on us by an official deed two estates, one called Villa Favières and the other, Voise.

58. Yet he exercised supreme power for only a brief time, however honorably and peaceably. His rule was ended by a premature death, and the kingship passed to Chlothar. This Chlothar, having heard of the fame of Blessed Maurus, frequently summoned him into his presence and wisely made use of his advice. Once Blessed Maurus sent two of the brothers to the king for certain necessities. After the king had generously granted all they had requested, he solicitously asked them about the grants his predecessors had bestowed on our house. When he heard their answer, he said, 'God willing, we will not deny our largess to the monastery, especially since by such gifts we gain greater power over both our realm and its wealth and obtain thereby God's good will'.

59. One day about this time, as Blessed Maurus was traveling about, putting the affairs of the abbey's estates in order, he stopped at one of its possessions called Jouy-sur-Morin, looking for a private place to rest. He had settled in and was chanting psalms with two monks who had accompanied him when it was announced that Ansegarius, archdeacon of the church of Angers, was outside and wished to speak

9. August 18th.

with him. The man of God directed him to enter, and the archdeacon explained to him the various issues he had come about. Then the holy Maurus called the monk Simplicius and said to him 'We ought to toast this man who has long since become our intimate owing to his reverence and affability with the cup of charity and intoxicate ourselves with the wine of holy affection spiritually, as spiritual men'. Simplicius however responded, 'We have no wine with us, except what is in a little saddlebag'. Maurus, holy to the Lord, said to him, 'Bring it here'. And when it had been brought to him, he added, 'bring the bread here as well'. When they had brought the bread to him, he made the sign of the cross over the little saddlebag, and said 'Mighty is God, who prepared a table in the desert and brought forth water in abundance from the rock and for us his servants will serve an abundance of wine from this small vessel'. A nearly incredible event followed, wonderful in the telling: Sixty men and more arrived who drank from that same vessel, three at a time. Yet it was found to be ever full, as if untouched after the first filling. Simplicius related this miracle to us when he returned to the monastery with Blessed Maurus, comparing him to Elisha, who long ago fed a crowd of workers with a few morsels of food.[10]

60. As he was returning to the monastery from that place, he encountered along the road a peasant with a cancer that stretched from his lip to his nose and had consumed most of his cheek. The man of God had compassion on his calamity and, making the sign of the cross over him, restored the man to pristine health.

61. Meanwhile [King] Chlothar came into Anjou and sent instructions to the man of God that he wished to visit the monastery. When he replied that he was welcome to come, the king made haste, bringing only a few attendants. When he arrived, the king granted to the monastery a royal fisc called Blaise and transferred to them by the same royal authority an estate known as Longchamp. When Blessed Maurus also asked that the king confirm by royal edict that the congregation of the abbey should forever conduct its own elections, he freely assented to the petition of the man of God by royal decree. Having received a blessing on his party, he then departed.

10. Cf. 2 Kgs 4:42-43.

Chapter ten: The death of the holy Maurus and his successors

62. Now from that time on, Blessed Maurus was quite reluctant to leave the monastery. Priors and other officials had been appointed and he had leisure for God alone in daily prayer and reading, and he devoted himself even more fervently than in his earlier days to monastic discipline. Observing that, day after day, his flock was also progressing in its observance of monastic life, he would offer most devoutly a sacrifice of rejoicing with praising lips to almighty God. In the thirty-eighth year since the foundation of the monastery, since he had both attained a perfected stage of life and, according to his master's prophecy, since he was to receive the recompense of his labors from the Lord after sixty years had passed, he understood that his life was approaching its end. So he took up a more secluded life in a small cell, which had been constructed for him next to the church of Blessed Martin.

63. Yet because the flock could not continue without a shepherd to direct it with all care, the holy man summoned the community and solicitously addressed the issue of a new abbot. The entire monastic community solemnly decided that the person should be chosen who better understood each monk than he understood himself. The holy father then determined that Bertulf, the very noble monk whom he himself had devoutly brought up and who had become perfected in the monastic life, was the proper person to undertake such a task. When the entire community had given assent to this choice, the most holy father appointed him to sit in the abbot's place. He then commended to his care with fatherly affection, one by one, each member of that large flock that was now his responsibility. He then withdrew into small cell that, as I said, had been built for him next to the church of Saint Martin. He had chosen two brothers from the community to live with and serve him, Primus and Anianus. Those of us who had originally accompanied him he commanded to remain close at hand to watch over Bertulf, whom he had constituted abbot, that he might not by some mischance deviate from the right path of the Rule.

64. He had completed two and a half years thus in contrition of spirit and mortification of body when one night, as was his custom, he went

alone to the church of Blessed Martin to fulfill his vow of prayers and tears to the Lord. But the devil, surrounded with a great crowd of minions, blocked his entry. He said, 'Woe unto you, Maurus, who came to these remote regions so long unknown to you and your kind, hoping to unseat us. Now, however, you shall endure both in seeing and experience a completely forsaken population from our invasion. I will revel in triumph over you and bring on such slaughter that it will seem that not one of that large and single-hearted community of yours has survived'. To him the man of the Lord replied, 'May the Lord rebuke you, Satan, and your words, for you are a liar and the father of falsehoods'. Immediately the enemy vanished with so great and terrible noise that it seemed to the man of God that the whole monastery shook on its foundation. Jolted awake by the noise, the brothers were stricken with fear; they arose at once, rang the bell, and began chanting the night office.

65. Meanwhile when the man of God, grieving with affliction and weariness beyond measure over what he had heard, went into the church of Blessed Martin, he besought the Lord to make clear to him the meaning of the evil spirit's word. Immediately an angel of the Lord, standing by him in a brilliant white garment, said, 'Soul so beloved of God, why are you burdened by such sorrow for what God has decreed must come to pass? Though the devil is indeed the source of all falsehood, he does have knowledge beforehand of many things, particularly such as often occur. His revelations to you, however, came not by his own will but by God's command. Thus what you have heard is the truth in every detail: The greater part of this community will, within a short time, be collected to the Lord, as has been set down and preordained. But Satan will not triumph by this as he claimed, even for a brief time. Prepared by your exhortations and admonitions, each one of the monks will await the day of his summons home with rejoicing. You will happily send on ahead those who are to die presently that you might thereby deserve to follow them with even greater joy.'

66. When this had been announced, the vision of an angel standing close by and speaking vanished. When morning had come, the holy man of God rehearsed to the entire community all that he had heard. With fatherly sollicitude, he then addressed them thus, 'Regarding

those things that the Lord's servants know that He wills: If they start lamenting, it would seem that, in that very sorrow, they oppose the will of God. And this is the reason: He has set down a limit to life for mortal men beyond which none can go. His never-changing wrath towards the first man who brought death to all has remained his judgment on all. But he has willed to reveal to us that the day of our death is close, so that we might wipe clean the stains of our offenses through tears of penitence and bodily mortification. Let us, as the prophet admonishes us, examine with care our ways and our works, and come before the Lord in confession that we may enter the gates of the heavenly city with hymns, professing our faith, and may, when his countenance has been revealed, thereby be found worthy to contemplate his glory with all the saints. Dearly beloved brothers, we know the time is now at hand when judgment shall come forth out of the house of the Lord. His judgments, which indeed are sometimes hidden, but never unjust, will be vindicated. Therefore let us persevere to the end, as befits the servants of the good Lord. Let us adore him, lifting up cheerful hearts, and let us take care that no imperfect action accuse us. Let us keep vigil attentively lest the tempter attack us from behind and overthrow us as we enter into this, the eleventh hour of our journey.

67. Strengthened by the holy man's exhortation, the community began to prepare itself with such steadfastness for the final hour to come that not one of them doubted that whoever departed this life in that monastery would ascend to a heavenly home. For it came to pass that within five months that one hundred sixty died there; out of such a large flock no more than twenty-four monks remained alive. Among them we buried Antony and Constantinianus, our comrades and companions. After such a great number had succumbed in that house, Blessed Maurus himself was afflicted by a grave pain in his side. He grew ever weaker and finally, lying on his bed of sackcloth before the altar of Saint Martin, he provided for his passage by receiving the life-giving sacraments. On the eighteenth day of the Kalends of February,[11] forty-five years after he had come to that place, with his remaining disciples surrounding him, he went happily to the Lord. He was buried in that same chapel on the right side of the altar. There, through

11. January 15th.

his merits and prayers, God worked many magnificent miracles to the praise and glory of his name.

68. After the holy man's passing, Simplicius and I resolved to return to our monastery—as he had commanded us to do on the day he died. The man of God Bertulf begged us not to depart during his lifetime. Because of his holiness we dared not offend him, so we remained there for two years until he died. Florianus, a man of perfect monastic observance and the son of our guide Harderadus, succeeded Bertulf in the rule of the monastery. He too had been bought up by Blessed Maurus and tried likewise to detain us with many prayers, but we returned to you, holy fathers, with God's guidance. Now, in compliance with your commands, we have committed to writing, admittedly in a rude style, these matters concerning the life of Blessed Maurus, his entry into monastic life and his miracles. The days of Blessed Maurus' life may be calculated thus: When he was twelve years old, he was offered to God and given over to Blessed Benedict; he remained with him for twenty years; he then resided in his own monastery, which he himself had built, for forty years and fourteen days; altogether these make up seventy-two years and fourteen days. By all these things may God be glorified, who reigns forever and ever. Amen.

The Death and Burial of Maurus. Paris: BNF MS Troyes 2273, f. 73v.
(Photo credit: Bibliothèque Nationale de France)

THE LITTLE BOOK OF MIRACLES

Maurus strikes down a despoiler of Glanfeuil. Paris, BNF MS Troyes 2273 fol. 77r. (Photo credit: Bibliothèque Nationale de France)

INTRODUCTION

The *Little Book of Miracles* of Blessed Maurus, translated below, is the companion piece to Abbot Odo's *Life of Maurus*. It is inscribed after the *Life* in a ninth century Bible known as the Rorigo Bible, and may be an autograph copy by Odo himself.[1] Unlike the *Life of Maurus*, which is attributed to a sixth-century contemporary of Blessed Maurus, this *Little Book of Miracles* is confessedly the work of Abbot Odo of Glanfeuil.

The text consists of a two-part history of Glanfeuil from about 750 to 868. The first section chronicles events at the abbey from the time of its donation to Gaidulf of Ravenna by Pepin the Short in the mid 700s through its restoration under Count Rorigo in the 830s and the subsequent tenure of its first abbot, Rorigo's nephew Gauzlinus. The second part consists of miracle stories, organized chronologically through Odo's own abbacy, which began in 861. This second part is itself divisible into two sections: the first contains miracles performed at Glanfeuil itself; the second recounts supernatural events which occurred during the translation of the relics of Maurus from Glanfeuil to the abbey of St. Pierre-des-Fossés in Paris, when the community took refuge there from the Vikings. A short conclusion describes the arrival

1. Bib. nat. MS. latin 3, ff. 402r-407r. The document has no title in the Rorigo Bible; this translation adapts the caption used in later manuscripts: The *Little Book of Miracles*. There is a modern, though partial, critical edition, which omits most of the miracle stories: *Ex Odonis Miraculis S. Mauri*, in Oswald Holder-Egger, ed., *Ex Adrevaldi Floriocensis miracles S. Benedicti*, MGH SS 15.1 (Hannover, 1887) 462-472. On the possibility that Bib. nat. latin 3 is an autograph copy by Abbot Odo, see *MCMA*, 2:970.

of the relics at Fossés and the climactic visit of King Charles the Bald to the saint's new shrine in 868. Unlike the fanciful *Life of Maurus*, the historical portions of the *Little Book of Miracles* constitute an overall credible account of Glanfeuil abbey and the development of the cult of Maurus from the mid-eighth through the late-ninth century.

The narrative opens around 755 with the carolingian king Pepin III's donation of the abbey to a rapacious military commander, Gaidulf of Ravenna. The grant was typical of the early carolingian policy of delivering over monastic lands to military allies.[2] Gaidulf received lordship over other angevin monastic lands as well, probably as a reward for supporting Pepin's recent successful campaign against the lombard kingdom in northern Italy.[3] While there is no reason to doubt the account of the ruination of the abbey under Gaidulf, Odo may have used the count's occupation to explain changes at the abbey which had less personal causes.[4] First, Odo notes that Gaidulf's persecution of the monks was so oppressive that they could no longer live the rigorous life prescribed by the Rule of Benedict, and so instead assumed the status of canons, eventually becoming clerics 'of the very lowest sort'.[5] As we have seen above, the notion that the community at Glanfeuil observed the Rule of Benedict since the time of the abbey's foundation in the 540s is likely a fabrication of Abbot Odo's *Life of Maurus*. Glanfeuil was probably only one among many monasteries that were abandoning the monastic life to become houses of secular canons status in the late eighth century. Some scholars suggest that such shifts did not imply any abandonment of standards, arguing that the exaltation of monastic life over that of canons developed only under late carolingian reformers.[6] Odo may have projected backwards preferences from his own times,

2. See above, *Introduction* to the *Life of Maurus*, note 32.

3. Pepin also granted Gaidulf lordship over the monasteries of Saint Lézin and Saint Aubin. Henri Leclercq (DACL, 6,1:1306) speculated that Gaidulf may have received the entire county of Anjou, in part on the grounds that Count Rorigo received the abbey of Glanfeuil as count of Anjou and lost it in 835 when he lost the office of count.

4. *MCMA*, 2:969.

5. *Little Book of Miracles*, section 8.

6. Mayke de Jong, 'Carolingian Monasticism: The Power of Prayer,' 631f.; and Martin Claussen, *The Reform of the Frankish Church* (Cambridge, Cambridge University Press, 2004) 30ff.

thereby also supporting his central fiction of the strict observance of the benedictine Rule at Glanfeuil from the mid-sixth century onwards.

Another likely distortion in this first section involves Gaidulf's destruction of the monastery's property. Odo contends that, in addition to his demolition of the monastery's buildings, the evil commander destroyed the documents that would have provided written proof of properties claimed by the abbey, boasting that as a result the monks could never regain their possessions through legal processes. This comment surely demonstrates the abbey's lack of written evidence of its claims to properties in Odo's times, when such documentation was becoming legally necessary.[7] Several other passages scattered throughout the *Little Book of Miracles* are intended to substantiate claims to certain privileges and properties. In paragraph 19, Archbishop Ebroin denies the claims of Fossés to rule over Glanfeuil because the written evidence of that grant by Emperor Louis the Pious had been stolen and destroyed.[8] In paragraphs 19 and 20, Odo carefully records the issuance of charters to archbishop Ebroin, establishing his lordship over the abbey. In paragraph 22, we read that, during the transfer of Blessed Maurus' relics, an ancient parchment was discovered confirming that the relics were indeed his, thus providing written support of the abbey's oral tradition. Mentioning the existence of charters was a common strategy of carolingian histories, designed in part to provide evidence for property claims, the written proof for which had either been lost or, as was often the case, had never existed.[9] Odo's repeated admonition to the reader to have complete faith in his narrative (paragraphs 5, 39, 41) may reflect the debatable nature of the abbey's claims.

7. R. McKitterick, *The Carolingians and the Written Word* (Cambridge: Cambridge University Press) 174f.

8. The suggestion that Ebroin himself destroyed this document seems unlikely, given the positive attitude towards the Rorigo family that Odo, himself a member of the clan, exhibits throughout the narrative. See L. Levillain, 'L'archichapelain Ebroin, évêque de Poitiers,' *Le Moyen Age* 34 (1923) 180.

9. For examples of this practice, see Head, *Hagiography and the Cult of the Saints*, 34ff. Perhaps to give verisimilitude to this account, Odo claims in paragraph 9 of the *Little Book of Miracles* that Gaidulf had hidden some of the documents, which Odo, after he became abbot, traced to the neighboring abbey of Saint Aubin only to find that they had been laid aside and later destroyed in a viking raid.

Some fifty years later, in the 830s, the abbey ruined by Gaidulf was restored by the pious Count Rorigo, a nobleman from Maine, and his spouse, Bildechildis. Descended from a prominent family of Maine,[10] Count Rorigo rose to still higher prominence in the ninth century owing to his liaison with Rotrud, one of the daughters of Charlemagne. By her, he had a son, Louis (d. 867), who later became abbot of Saint Denis near Paris and arch-chancellor to Charles the Bald. After Rotrud died in 810, Rorigo married a certain Bildechildis. By her he had at least six children who rose high in the later carolingian central government and in regional politics. They included Gauzlinus, who succeeded his half-brother, Louis, as arch-chancellor to Charles the Bald, and later became archbishop of Paris.[11] Others of his relatives ruled over the abbey of Glanfeuil until the community fled before the Vikings in the early 860s. Rorigo's younger brother, Gauzbert, a monk of Saint-Pierre-des-Fossés near Paris, was Glanfeuil's first superior, and his two sons (likely conceived before he entered monastic life), Gauzlinus and Theodradus, followed him as abbots of Glanfeuil. Count Rorigo's cousin, or perhaps nephew, Ebroin, obtained the lordship of Glanfeuil in 847 and was later appointed bishop of Poitiers and abbot of Saint Germain-des-Prés.

Rorigo's new wife, Bildechildis, may in fact have been the moving force behind the restoration of the abbey, given her enthusiasm for embracing the religious life and for rebuilding the abbey (paragraph 12). After the Count's death, she became an abbess (paragraph 5), and it has been suggested that Glanfeuil had originally been her property.[12] The

10. Roger, Count of Le Mans under Charles Martel, was likely Rorigo's great-grandfather, and Gauziolinus, a major eighth-century bishop of Le Mans, was likely his grand uncle: K.S.B. Keats-Rohan, 'Two Studies in North French Prosopography' in the *Journal of Medieval History* 20, (1994) 6. Another branch of this family may have held the counties of Meaux and Laon; if so, these families were related to the Carolingians themselves through the marriage of Bertrada, daughter of Charlibert of Laon, to Pepin III; See Keats-Rohan, 'Two Studies', note 22. Jacques Boussard, 'Les destineées de la Neustrie du ix au xi siècle', *Cahiers de civilization* 11 (1968) 19.

11. As evidence of the family's importance, see Janet Nelson, ed. and trans., *Annals of Saint Bertin* (Manchester: Manchester University Press) 86: when Gauzlinus and his half brother Louis were captured by pirates, in 857, their huge ransom was paid by a coalition of ecclesiastics and lay magnates of Neustria.

12. *MCMA*, 2:970.

pious couple took as much care for the spiritual renewal of the abbey as for its physical restoration. A number of monks were brought down from the Parisian abbey of Fossés to populate the new foundation. The group included Count Rorigo's brother, Gauzbertus, who had held a high position in the world before he embraced monastic life (paragraph 17). Odo praises him for his monastic zeal. Gauzbertus seems to have become the ruler of monastery shortly after arriving there, but did not hold the title of abbot (paragraphs 17, 18, 24). He likely served as a prior under the abbot of Fossés, to whom—in order to maintain monastic zeal there—Count Rorigo had entrusted the oversight of the foundation in perpetuity. It is, however, possible that Odo fabricated this section on Fossés in order to emphasize the unity of the two communities, which were joined together under his abbacy in 668.

In 835, Louis the Pious transferred the lordship of the angevin abbeys to his son, Pepin.[13] At that point, Count Rorigo engineered the transfer of the lordship of Glanfeuil to his relative, Ebroin.[14] The latter was at the time a young cleric on the rise, who would later have a role in carolingian royal politics as bishop of Poitiers and abbot of Saint Germain-des-Près. Odo claims that the transfer of Glanfeuil to Ebroin stemmed primarily from Count Rorigo's concern to maintain strict monastic observance at Glanfeuil and in order 'that the foundation might not fall into alien hands . . . as had happened before' (paragraph 19). This comment hints at the probable reality: that Count Rorigo lost the lordship of Glanfeuil along with all his other royal offices as a result of his support of Lothair's rebellion against the emperor Louis the Pious in 833. Ebroin, however, had remained faithful to the emperor. So Rorigo managed to get his lost lordship of Glanfeuil transferred to a relative, thus keeping his beloved foundation in the family.[15]

13. For this date, *MCMA*, 2:970.

14. A full account of Ebroin's career is presented in Levillain (note 7 above). There is no clear evidence for the claim that he was Count Rorigo's cousin, a suggestion tentatively supported by *MCMA,* 2: 970. *The Little Book of Miracles* (section 19) simply defines the relationship as *consanguineus . . . affinitate carnalis generositatis.*

15. J. Smith: 'Culte imperial et politiques frontière dans la valle de la Viliane' in *Landévennec et le monachisme breton dans le haut moyen age* (Association Landévennec, 1985) 131; see also Jean-Pierre Brunterc'h, 'Le duché du Maine et la marche de Bretagne,' in Hartmut Atsma, ed., *La Neustrie.* (Sigmaringen: J. Thorbecke, 1989) 1:60-61.

After Rorigo's death, Ebroin, now the powerful bishop of Poitiers, strengthened the family's position by challenging the right of Fossés to govern Glanfeuil. The document conferring that authority, according to Odo, had been 'stolen and committed to the fire' (paragraph 20). Some historians have suggested that Ebroin was himself the agent of its destruction.[16] Then, in 844, Ebroin used his growing influence at court obtain from Charles the Bald a charter that raised the foundation to the status of an independent abbey, with typical monastic immunities (paragraph 21).[17] He completed his family's absorption of Glanfeuil by obtaining a royal grant ordering that the abbot always be a member of the Rorigo family, so long as a suitable candidate was available. Finally, Ebroin obtained from Charles the Bald the appointment of Gauzlinus, 'the son of Gauzbertus', as the first formally installed abbot since Count Rorigo's restoration (paragraph 23).[18]

16. See note 7 above.

17. For the date, see Bloch, *MCMA*, 2: 971; McKitterick, *The Frankish Kingdoms under the Carolingians*, 181; *Recueil des actes de Charles le Chauve*, 3:231f.; Paul Marchegay 'Le donation d'Anouuareth', *Annales de Bretagne* 9 (1894) 216-37; Levillain, 'L'archichapelain Ebroin', 200. Normally the temporal estates of carolingian abbeys were under the authority of the king: Head, *Hagiography*, 29. Glanfeuil's rival abbey, Fleury, had obtained immunities from Louis the Pious: Head, *Hagiography*, 30.

18. There is some confusion about the identity of this person. Herbert Bloch, who has recently studied this text, accepts this identification as literally true. Bloch (*MCMA*, 2:971) asserts that Gauzbertus, the brother of Count Rorigo and the first ruler of the restored abbey of Glanfeuil, had two sons, Gauzlinus and Theodradus, both of whom served in turn as abbots of Glanfeuil. However, all commentators agree that Count Rorigo and Bilechildis also had a son of that name, who was given as an oblate to Glanfeuil in 839. Earlier historians assert that this Gauzlinus was abbot of Glanfeuil and that the term 'son of Gauzbertus' described a spiritual rather than blood relationship; see Levillain, 'L'archichapelain Ebroin', 183, note 3; Paul Marchegay, 'Cartulaire de Saint-Maur-sur-Loire', *Archives d'Anjou* 1 (1843) 378, note 34. Bloch, however, insists this is a different person, who left Glanfeuil to succeed his half brother, Louis, as arch-chancellor to Charles the Bald and ended his life as bishop of Paris. One would have to presume, on Bloch's reading, that Gauzbertus fathered two sons before entering the monastic life. This is not unreasonable, since Odo is careful to note (*Little Book of Miracles*, paragraph 17) that Gauzbertus had enjoyed a high position 'in the world' before embracing a monastic vocation. Bloch's reasoning accounts for all the persons involved, though the Rorigid tendency to reuse a few names leaves this identification in some uncertainty.

The abbacy of Gauzlinus clearly marks a major transition in the cult of Maurus at Glanfeuil. Odo comments that once he was appointed abbot, the monastery 'began to advance nobly in monastic devotion and appeared second to none in its day as regards devotion to divine worship' (paragraph 21). Noting that he is following the learned abbot's own narrative, Odo recounts that shortly after Gauzlinus became abbot (March 845), he solemnly transferred Maurus' relics to a more prominent place in the abbey church. In the process, he discovered ancient documents proving the identity of the bones as those of Maurus. He also uncovered relics of Saints Stephen and Peter, which associated the abbey's patron (a deacon, according to the *Life of Maurus*) with the first deacon and martyr of the church, as well as with Peter, with whom Maurus had shared both the ability to walk on water and the role of immediate successor to a great founder. Gauzlinus' actions here have led two modern writers to describe him as the founder of the cult of Maurus at Glanfeuil.[19] It was just at this time that the cults of Benedict and Scholastica were being intensively developed at the nearby abbeys of Fleury and Le Mans.

Odo's detailed narrative of Gauzlinus' abbacy further highlights his centrality in the development of the restored abbey. Odo carefully noted the abbot's ordination to the deaconate and priesthood and dwelt upon Gauzlinus' intellectual abilities. This convinced Charles the Bald to appoint him abbot (paragraph 21). Gauzlinus also produced a 'detailed account' of the transfer of Maurus' relics, from which Abbot Odo says he drew his own narrative (paragraph 22). Finally, in the second section of the *Little Book of Miracles*, which recounts the miracles of Maurus, Odo notes that more of these wonders occurred under Gauzlinus than during any other abbacy, including his own.

Gauzlinus was succeeded in 853 by his brother, Theodradus, who ruled for eight years, until 861.[20] These years witnessed increasing danger

19. *MCMA*, 2:971. Leclercq, 'Glanfeuil', 1304. Only one document that predates Gauzlinus' 'discoveries' connect Maurus with Glanfeuil. This is a charter of only two years earlier which mentions, 'The monastery of Glanna, where rest the bodily remains of the blessed confessor of Christ, Maurus.' This charter does not identify Maurus with Benedict, and its date and authenticity are not firmly established: Marchegay, 'Cartulaire de St-Maur-sur-Loire', #34.

20. For the date, see *MCMA*, 2:972.

from viking invasions and increasing disorder within the kingdom. The violence surrounding the two miracles which Odo recounts from Theodradus' abbacy reflect this growing unrest (paragraphs 33 and 34).

Odo himself succeeded Theodradus as abbot of Glanfeuil in 861. Modern scholars have concluded that Odo was also member of the Rorigo family, owing primarily to his reference to 'our family' when speaking of the Rorigids in paragraph 20.[21] This supposition is strengthened by the earlier decree of Charles the Bald that the abbots of Glanfeuil be drawn from the Rorigid family whenever possible. No other evidence regarding Odo's personal history has survived.

As if to emphasize the foundational importance of Gauzlinus' abbacy, Odo ends the narrative of the restoration of Glanfeuil with his death. At that point Odo takes up an account of the miracles that Maurus performed for his revived congregation. The abbacies of Gauzlinus' two successors, his brother Theodradus and Odo himself, are mentioned only in the context of these miracles, which differ significantly from those described in the *Life of Maurus*. In the earlier parts of this narrative diseases were cured or wounds healed by the prayers of the living Maurus—which emphasized Maurus' imitation of his model and patron, Benedict; later miracles, modelled on Christ's healing miracles rather than Benedict's, emphasized his independent status. The miracles described in the *Little Book of Miracles*, on the other hand, are posthumous and therefore serve different purposes. First, there were the miracles performed at Glanfeuil itself: Odo described these as 'the distinctive signs of the divine power that were displayed in this monastery through this blessed personage' (paragraph 23). In her study of medieval miracles, Benedicta Ward has referred to such phenomena as 'vengeance stories'.[22] The patron saint intervenes when some violence is visited upon his monastic community or his property: the ruthless military captain Gaidulf oppresses the monks and destroys the abbey (paragraphs 8-10); strongmen try to seize goods entrusted to the abbey for safekeeping (paragraphs 24-25, 33); an evil nobleman kills one of the abbey's servants (paragraph 31); a monastic tax is usurped (paragraph 32). In each of these cases, the monastic community prays

21. See 'Historical Introduction to the Life of Blessed Maurus' above, note 33.

22. Benedicta Ward, *Miracles and the Medieval Mind: Theory, Record and Event, 1000–1215* (Philadelphia: University of Pennsylvania Press, rev. ed., 1987) 49.

to Maurus for help and in each case retribution is swift. In the case of Gaidulf, Maurus physically attacks the despoiler of the monastery with fatal results; in other cases, the saint's vengeance is accomplished more indirectly: a sudden rainstorm literally washes away robbers (paragraph 25); a predator falls ill and dies, spewing out excrement (paragraph 31); a third thief was seized by demons from a boat he had stolen from the abbey, and his intestines were ripped out (paragraph 33); yet another is beaten by a friend inspired by a sense of outraged justice (paragraph 32); other assailants of the monastery are imprisoned or executed by the Normans (paragraph 34). Such stories, as modern scholars have frequently pointed out, helped to protect the persons and property of monasteries in an unsettled age. Often the only defense religious establishments could mount was the fear that such stories might inspire in potential oppressors.[23] The saint protected his community from natural disasters as well: the custodian of Maurus' main church at Glanfeuil was miraculously (and amusingly) tricked into leaving his sleeping chamber just before it collapsed (paragraph 29).

The two most elaborately narrated miracles at Glanfeuil have a quite different character, however. The first (paragraphs 26, 27) involves a noble visitor from Brittany who had a vision of Maurus carrying the liturgical prayers of the community to an angel who then transported them to the throne of God. Odo then recounts a similar phenomenon that had occurred several years later: during the night office, the entire community heard an angelic choir singing and saw a heavenly light suffusing the entire monastery as a host of angels joined the monks in keeping vigil before the holy relics of Maurus. Such miracles pressed the point that the presence of Maurus' relic made Glanfeuil a focus of divine splendor and power.

A similar message is conveyed by the second group of miracles, those that occurred during the 'translation' of the founder's relics from Glanfeuil to the abbey of Fossés in Paris in the 860s. These were all curative rather than 'vengeance miracles' and demonstrated that the power of the saint was not confined to his burial place. As Odo himself stated: 'the body of the holy saint is as often visited and honored by the heavenly hosts wherever it is carried as it is at its tomb' (paragraph 37). These wonders all occurred among the large crowds that followed

23. Ward, *Miracles and the Medieval Mind*, esp. 44ff.

the relics in their long, wandering journey from Glanfeuil to Paris, and thereby manifested the growing popularity and power of the saint.

Two of these wonders provided particularly telling examples of Maurus' curative powers even away from his shrine at Glanfeuil. In the first (paragraph 36), a woman cured of vomiting blood has a vision of heavenly choirs singing ethereal melodies as they keep watch before the temporary shrine of Maurus' relics; this parallels the saint's 'epiphanies' at his shrine at Glanfeuil (recounted above in paragraph 28). In the second miracle sixteen nobles were cured who had suffered from lameness, blindness, deafness or an inability to speak (paragraph 40). This cure, Odo carefully notes, repeats an earlier miracle at Glanfeuil by which eight persons were cured of the same afflictions (paragraph 23). Apparently Maurus' powers could expand, even as his relics moved further away from his home shrine.[24]

The *Little Book of Miracles* reaches its climax with the visit of King Charles the Bald to the relics after they had been enthroned at the Parisian monastery of Fossés (paragraph 41). There the ruler of the western carolingian lands proclaims himself the devotee of Saint Maurus, offering rich liturgical gifts to the shrine in the hope of attaining salvation 'through the holy one's intercession.'[25]

Odo's account transformed what must have been for his community a journey of great difficulty, anxiety, and dispossession into a triumphant procession of the relics of Maurus through crowds of admiring devotees, many cured of their ailments, to its culmination in the homage rendered to Maurus from the ruler of the western empire. At this dramatic point, Odo fittingly ended his *Little Book of Miracles* with a brief prayer for God's mercy through Maurus' intercession.

Odo was elected abbot of the newly combined monastic congregations of Fossés and Glanfeuil in Paris and ruled over them until his death some years later.[26] His election was surely a testimony to the

24. However, in two miracles which occurred during the translation of the relics, the sick person had to spend the entire night in the presence of the relics to effect their cures (sections 36, 39). For a discussion of 'incubation' miracles, see Head, *Hagiography*, 166.

25. Fossés was the 'family monastery' of Charles' empress, Ermentrude: J. Nelson, *Charles the Bald* (New York: Longmans, 1992) 205. His visit may have immediately preceded or followed her death in 869.

26. *Gallia Christiana* (Paris, 1744) 7:287.

energy and creativity which is also evident in the writings whereby he celebrated his patron. His election was also likely a consequence of the cult he had brought to the relatively obscure monastery of Fossés. Maurus soon replaced Saint Peter as the patron of the parisian abbey, and Fossés became the centre of a cult of Maurus that spread to most european benedictine houses in the following centuries.[27] The parisian abbey refused to return the relics to Glanfeuil after the viking incursions ended, and so Maurus' original home on the Loire decayed into a minor priory, its extensive properties long lost and its attraction to pilgrims gone.[28] Although Glanfeuil survived the French Revolution, it was forced to close in 1901 by the anti-clerical french government. Its few remaining monks moved to the abbey of Clervaux in Luxembourg, of which Blessed Maurus now serves as a patron.

The abbey of Fossés, on the other hand, prospered throughout the Middle Ages as the repository of the relics of Maurus. In 1750, however, these were transferred to the abbey church of Saint Germain-des-Prés, the center of a religious and scholarly reform movement named after Maurus: the Congrégation de Saint-Maur.[29] The relics remained there until, after having been preserved through so many vicissitudes of history, they were strewn about the neighborhood streets by adherents of the French Revolution. Even so, devotion to Blessed Maurus and belief in his curative powers continues to this day both within the Benedictine Order and among faithful laity.[30]

27. Though the abbey's new name, Saint-Maur-des-Fossés, was commonly used from the late ninth century, it was not formally altered until the thirteenth century: *Gallia Christiana* 7:282ff.

28. Glanfeuil may have produced wine of some significance. The first mention of the famous *chenin* grape occurs at Glanfeuil in the ninth century: www.itvfrance.com/regions/documents/1/Biblio%20Chenin%202002.pdf.

29. Barbara Dilam, *Les Sculptures medievales de Saint-Maur-des-Fossés* (Saint-Maur: Société d'Histoire et d'Archéologie, 1983), 23.

30. www.osb.org/gen/maurus/maurlife.htm, the official American benedictine website, contains a modern life and set of devotions to Blessed Maurus; a catholic devotional website contains a modern litany to Saint Maurus: www.catholicculture.org/lit/Prayers/view.cfm?id=1165.

LITTLE BOOK OF MIRACLES

OF THE PRESENT TIME, WHICH THE DIVINE MAJESTY WILLED TO WORK THROUGH BLESSED MAURUS, SET DOWN IN GOOD FAITH BY ABBOT ODO[1]

1. This translation follows the oldest MS copy, the so-called Rorigo Bible (Bibliotheque national, MS Latin 3, fols 402r-406v). This bible was presented to the abbey by its restorer, Count Rorigo and carried from Glanfeuil to the abbey of Fossés in 869, as the community fled with the relics of Maurus before the Viking invaders. At some point about this time, the *Life of Maurus* and the *Little Book of Miracles of Blessed Maurus* were added to the bible text. Odo says in section seven that he composed the latter text in 868. For a discussion of the manuscript, see H. Bloch, *Monte Cassino in the Middle Ages* (Harvard University Press, 1986) 2:1026. There is a good modern edition, which however omits several of the miracles: *Ex Odonis miraculis s. Mauri in Ex Adrevaldi Floriocensis miraculis S. Benedicti*, ed. Oswald Holder-Egger, Monumenta Germaniae Historica, Scriptores 15.1 (Hannover, 1887) 462-472.

5. I often remember your[2] request that I attempt in good faith to collect and order in the compass of a little volume the history of the destruction and restoration of the holy monastery that was long ago worthily constructed by the Blessed Maurus, from olden times called Glanfeuil. I learned this story from venerable and virtuous persons still alive today, and I have judged it fitting to insert their names at the beginning of the narrative that I may thereby remove from readers any unease of doubt. I also invite all who listen to embrace in its integrity what I narrate truly and faithfully as pleasing to both God and man. First and foremost among them both in high rank and in perfect holiness of life, stands Godefridus, venerable abbot of the abbey of Fossés, who lived in that holy community for a lengthy period under the rule of Theodradus of holy memory. Then there is Abbess Bilechildis, now specially honored in her holy widowhood. She, along with her husband, the illustrious Count Rorigo, carefully supervised the rebuilding of the monastery over many years in accord with what was revealed to them and commanded from on high. Through frequent discussions with her, I learned much of what I narrate here. The priest Bernegar stands third among these: no one in our community who knows his wholly admirable life, especially his zeal for holy prayer, could ever doubt the truth of his information whom we honor as our venerable father of earlier times. He had lived for twelve years continuously in this monastery, first under Gauzlinus of pious memory and afterwards with Gauzlinus' brother Theodradus, named above.

2. This translation uses the section numbers of the easily available text in the *Acta Sanctorum: Historia translationis auctore Odone abate AA SS* (Antwerp, 1643-) 1:1051-1060. The four sections preceding section 5, with which this text begins, contain the Letter of Odo of Glanfeuil to Archdeacon Adelmodus, which, following the arrangement of the original manuscript of the *Little Book of Miracles* in the 'Rorigo Bible', has been translated at the beginning of the *Life of Blessed Maurus*, above, pp. 59-61.

3. The work is addressed to Adelmodus, archdeacon of Le Mans.

6. To these witnesses were joined most of the brothers of the shrine, who stated they had been many times overcome with fear at the miracles worked in their day: the revelations and visitations from above, the music of ethereal, ineffable sweetness, and the angelic appearances, especially when these occurred during the nighttime hours. They claimed that their spirits had been many times so captivated by such sweetness that, with their hearts so intent on absorbing the sweet-sounding music and modulated tones, nothing except the halls of such overwhelming harmonies could remain in their breasts. From these stories I will describe a few in detail, as opportunity may occur for determining their essential points.

7. The course of this narrative begins at the time of Pepin, of revered memory, and continues up to our own time in the present year, which is 868 from the Incarnation of the Lord. In this year, by order of the serene king Charles, we transported with fitting ceremony, amidst a dense and numerous assembly, the holy remains of the body of the most blessed man into the monastery of the holy Mother of God the ever virgin Mary and of Blessed Peter, prince of the apostles (that in antiquity had been called Fossés). The saintly bishop, Aeneas, received the relics at the entry to the monastery with his own hands and, accompanied by a crowd of venerable monks and a throng of noble canons in the vestments and accoutrements of church ministers, brought them into the church of Blessed Peter with festive ceremonies and a solemn office of holy devotion. He then enclosed the relics in a metal receptacle that had been prepared. They are, by the help of God, now venerated here with fitting and continuous service by the monks, to the praise and honor of the Lord's name. He thus in our own time exalts his holy ones, to whom he has granted the everlasting rewards of heavenly joys, conforming them to and making them coheirs with his only Son. By his merits and interventions, we are made worthy to obtain forgiveness of our shameful sins and can boast of our redemption by the shedding of the holy blood of Christ.

HERE ENDS THE PREFACE

THE TEXT OF THE BOOK BEGINS

8. [*c.* AD 755] Until the reign of the glorious king Pepin, the observance of monastic discipline was perfectly maintained in that holy monastery. It rejoiced in having honor and dignity and a great abundance of all things. It also housed the number of monks that had been set down by Blessed Maurus. At that point, however, the excellent king gave the monastery, with all the possessions pertaining thereto, to a certain Gaidulf of Ravenna. Loosing the barbarism of his savage spirit and the harshness of his wild cruelty, this man began to persecute the monks living there with a deadly hatred. Because they could not endure the monstrous oppression, they fled, scattering all around the neighborhood. In the end only fourteen of the original number remained. Compelled by their unfortunate impoverishment, and too weak to do otherwise, they were barely able to beg a daily sustenance from that tyrant; still they continued, as best they could, to keep watch over the relics of the blessed saint. But when they were weakened as much by the hunger of famine as by the harsh suffering of their other miseries, they were no longer able to lead the rigorous life provided for by the holy Rule. So, after discussing the matter, they put aside their monastic garments for the vestments of canons. Whereupon that evil man in his tyrannical perversity used this opportunity to expel them all. He kept only five clerics, men of the lowest sort, for celebrating some sort of divine liturgy before the relics of the holy man. Then, prompted by his satanic master, he set about ruining the entire monastery. He even dug up the foundations of several buildings, as will be clear to anyone inspecting them today, as the gouged out substructures of various workshops are still visible. In the end he did not spare even the church buildings of that holy place, saying, 'As the Lord ordered the slaughter of the killing to begin at his holy place, [Cf. Ezk 9:6] so the ruination of my demolition will begin in the holy places and move boldly to the remaining structures'.

9. After doing all this, he carefully searched out all the documents regarding donation of the assets of the shrine. Adding bad to worse, some of these he burned, others he threw into the Loire, and several

others he placed in the monastery of Saint Aubin for safekeeping. Now when, in our own day, I learned about this, I went into the district of Anjou and approaching Prior Anscherius, begged him with many prayers that, if he knew those documents were among the archives or charters of his monastery, he would agree to return them to me. But the prior said, 'I confess that I did find documents of that sort when I was reviewing the laws of the old kings; but because no one ever came to enquire about these things, and I placed little value on them, they were put back with a cache of documents in the archive where they were first found. When the records of our own deeds and charters were destroyed by the persecution of the pagan invaders, your books perished along with them'.

10. Even so, I have compassion for that wretch, Gaidulf, quite aside from the avenging blow of condemnation which, by the just judgment of God, was to fall on him for having dared to carry out deeds of such enormous presumption. After he had—God permitting it—carried out against the foundation all the outrages he had conceived in his heart, he gathered together a crowd of friends and neighbors for the debauch of a most sumptuous feast. After an endless consumption of luxurious foods and an excessive drinking of unmixed wine, he began to recount to those present the deeds he had so wickedly done. Helplessly sunk into a pit of swaggering, he began to recall them, saying, 'No abominable species of monks spurred on by vain hopes will be able to bring suit and reclaim this abbey, for the documents by which they might think to recover possession of such a great estate perished in the destruction of the plundered houses'. He had not yet finished these words, when, all of a sudden, opposite him above the table at which he was still wantonly reclining, he saw standing a man dressed as a venerable monk. His countenance shone with a fiery aspect and his white hair glittered brighter than snow in the perfectly elegant dignity of its grandeur. He grasped a rod in his hand, and for a long moment he gazed at the miserable man with fierce eyes. Then the apparition struck Gaidulf in the gut with his foot with great force and then stoutly on the head with the rod. Immediately rendered senseless, his head snapping back and forth above his shoulders, Gaidulf cried out, wailing, 'Maurus, you are killing me! Maurus, you are murdering me!' Blinded by the blows to his head, he repeated these words to

those who were standing around listening. Finally, he ended his unhappy life, fittingly punished by the condemnation of unhappy Arius: his intestines burst and he shared the fate of demons.

11. Gerrannus, a monk of our monastery, swears that this is how things happened. He confirmed that he had often heard from his uncle, a monk of the same house, that the events occurred just as they have been described here. That same Gaidulf, in his perverted spirit, had expelled Gerrannus' uncle along with the rest of the brothers from the monastery. He came often to the house of his brother (that is, Gerrannus' father) and used to tell it over and over again. Devout older persons who have survived from then to our own time also attest to this story, very precisely filling in the details. Of these I interviewed two: I called them in for this purpose and carefully questioned them on all the issues. They asserted that these events were absolutely true, just as they had seen them with their own eyes. They added these details: after the expulsion of the inhabitants of the monastery and the deadly striking down of the evil Gaidulf, the count of Anjou and other men of arrogant and greedy spirit unjustly invaded and took possession of the estates and villas whose aids and payments had always sustained the monastery. This happened on that occasion because no one took the trouble to bring these things, as they had occurred, to the notice of his august majesty, the great emperor Charles.

12. [AD 830] After the monastery had been almost deserted and reduced to a wasteland, it, along with a small number of villas—being then the home of wild beasts[3]—was bestowed by the emperor on Count Rorigo of pious and happy memory, during the reign of the devout Augustus Louis. Since his heart had been touched by the inspiration of God and guided by the grace of divine favor, Count Rorigo, along with his wife, Bilechildis, began to search out how he might obtain perfection under a monastic rule by renouncing the world, freed from all secular occupation. He wondered how he might practically carry out his resolution. As his venerable wife agreed with the

4. Lit: 'as it was held by the onager'. The term *onager* (wild donkey) had been used in monastic circles since the time of Gregory the Great to symbolize the desert life of the hermit. See Gregory the Great, *Moralia in Job* 30.15.

project and promised to do the same, in accordance with her sex, they took pains to investigate the suitability of places where they could—with divine help—carry this out. But almighty God had decided not only to reform that monastery to its original rigor; he also willed to make these pious spouses known to men to reward their expenditures, freely undertaken as patronage of the monastery they were restoring. Accordingly, one day he touched the hearts of them both with the force of a holy desire to travel to the relics of Blessed Maurus for the purpose of prayer. Filled with the fervor of holy devotion, they mounted their horses and hastened from their home, which is called Le Bois, to render [Maurus] due homage. Once they had examined the place and settled on everything needed to make the abbey flourish with suitable distinction, they took especially careful counsel together on how to fashion its reconstruction. They immediately sent to Tours and summoned Lambert, a man of saintly life, from the monastery of the holy bishop Martin, and also Ebbo, a man of sufficient strength and one of their relatives. The venerable Count Rorigo then revealed his plans to them. Stirred to greater ardor by their discussions and mutual exhortations, they began with the greatest zeal to build the monastery: the foundations were laid to the satisfaction of the two men whom they had called forth.

13. But after they had been occupied for some time at accomplishing such a great task, they were delayed by certain problems, and the Rorigos went off to their very extensive breton holdings. There, for some time they made up various reasons for delay, and, owing to their absence, the work they had begun did not proceed. At that very time, a figure wearing a shimmering white monk's habit appeared to the abbot of the abbey of Cormery, James by name, who was entreating God with persistent prayers after the morning office, as was his custom. Standing near him, the figure with glowing countenance and milky white hair spoke thusly, 'Go out to the lands of Brittany, and seek out Count Rorigo. When you find him, explain to him these things that heaven has made known to you, "You are not acting rightly for a man with good intentions, since you are weighed down by the sluggishness of an unheeding spirit; you are entangled in the details of worldly affairs and so continue to direct your efforts towards transitory, passing matters that what you had intended to carry out, inspired by heavenly

desires, has been neglected. If you want God to be pleased with you and to help you—as you did only a short time ago—you must resume with the utmost zeal the project that you piously undertook but perilously put aside. By doing so you will, by God's gift, possess the merits of the wise man who built his house upon a rock,[4] and deserve to be made a heir to the heavenly kingdom along with Paul, the wise builder."'[5] The abbot replied, 'But I do not know this Rorigo. What is more, I do not know you, who are ordering such things.' But the heavenly vision repeated, 'Hurry! Seek him out as quickly as you can. As for who I am, you will know when it pleases the heavenly Creator.' Having said these things, the vision disappeared. Now the abbot was amazed at what he had seen and heard and did not want to reveal it to anyone. Instead he anxiously waited to see what might happen. A week went by and again the same figure appeared to him, at the same hour and in the same garments. He rebuked the abbot severely for neglecting to carry out what he had been ordered to do. The figure warned him to decide whether he would comply quickly with what he had heard. Yet still the abbot would not set his mind to carrying out what had been shown to him, holding back with a stubbornness beyond all reason, but suddenly a third time the figure stood again in the same place, heaping terrible abuse on the abbot, then striking him forcibly three times on his back with a painful scourge just as the abbot was about to sit down and threatening the abbot with death if he presumed to delay any longer in carrying out what had been ordered. The abbot suffered excruciatingly from the beating, since the heavenly lash had cut right through the softness of his skin "to the bone," as it is said, penetrating to his very marrow. Thoroughly terrified by the fear of imminent death, the abbot hastened to accomplish what had been commanded so harshly.

14. After making his way down many a long road, the abbot arrived in Brittany as he had hoped, ending a laborious journey. He was announced to Count Rorigo, and as he entered his presence the abbot

5. Mt 7:24.

6. 1 Cor 3:10: According to the commission of God given to me, like a skilled master-builder (*sapiens architectus*) I laid a foundation, and another man is building upon it. Let each man take care how he builds upon it. [RSV]

asked for a more private interview, indicating that he had been sent for a special purpose. Without further ado, the abbot began quickly to explain himself. The count thought him insane and attempted to silence him by protests. The abbot replied, 'Oh, most just of men, I am not insane, as you think. Rather I hope to confirm for you by clear evidence that I bear commands from a heavenly oracle.' Having said this, and weeping copiously, he uncovered his back and showed the count the livid stripes. He then told him everything that had transpired. When Count Rorigo's wife, whom he had summoned, came in, the abbot repeated everything and showed her as well the wounds of the divine scourging. They were astonished by these wonders and anxiously began discussing how to supervise with more care the work they had begun. They kept the abbot with them for two weeks, lavishing attention on him and ordering the frequent application of unguents. After his wounds healed over, they summoned him to their presence and promised to obey the divine instructions in every way. Then they sent him back to his abbey, rejoicing with a light heart and with many gifts. They themselves determined to set out for Anjou.

15. After they had turned off into a place called Verne to stay the night, the countess, who was pregnant, was suddenly taken ill. She was so severely stricken that everyone present feared for her life. The noble count, her husband, promptly took account of her situation and arranged for her to get to their destination quickly on horseback, distraught at the prospect of perhaps having to bury his spouse. As the count was later crossing the Loire by boat, his vessel seemed to drift in the midst of the stream when suddenly, a fiery sphere in the shape of a broad shield sent down from heaven appeared above him. He so clearly felt the strength of its heat that he feared the hair on his head would be consumed. His astonishment redoubled at what he was experiencing as he heard the utterance of a heavenly voice speaking in this fashion, 'Build here, build here, build here! Unless you solemnly undertake to act in a godly fashion, you will never again enjoy the sweet embraces of the spouse you sent away or attain in prosperity the term of years you have been allotted.' Experiencing all this alone in a boat in the middle of the river and committing himself to carry out everything, as soon as the boat docked he began to walk very quickly on dry land; with the fervor of true commitment, he quickly arrived at the shrine of Blessed

Maurus, for he had crossed the river not far from that place, perhaps two hundred paces, as one might reckon it. At the same hour—as afterwards they discovered in discussing what had transpired—his wife, who for three days and nights had lain without taking food or water, was freed from her serious illness; and when she had been carried to the same place in the identical vessel, without anyone's assistance she approached the shrine of the holy man filled with religious zeal.

16. At this time, a certain Bertingus, of a not inconsequential family, along with his wife Huninga, held the site in benefice [from the Rorigos]. Both the count and his wife therefore, having tarried there out of love and respect for the site, decided to return to Boscum, their usual residence. There, one day, after the morning office, as the venerable count was lingering in the little oratory, which he had devoutly constructed (as is the custom of more noble men) and where he would apply his mind to divine matters—as was his quite praiseworthy custom—through contemplation by means of psalms and prayers, there appeared standing near him an unknown figure who spoke this way: 'Delay no longer with regard to those matters which have been announced to you from above. For after the death of the Emperor Louis the times will not be so favorable as now for you to pursue the divine commands. Also, so that your spouse may be able more fully to recover from the discomfort in her shoulders and arm, a cluster of thirsty leeches should be applied to her'. Having said these things, it departed.

17. Immediately summoning his wife, the count rehearsed to her all that he had witnessed in detail. They immediately sent word, recalling Lambert and Ebbo. The couple repeated what had happened and had been revealed to them. All together they praised and blessed God for it, and the two men exhorted the noble couple to carry forward with great zeal, as best they could, the rest of the rebuilding project—which indeed they had begun so well but (according to the heavenly message the noble couple had received) had left unfinished through great negligence. Complying with the counsel they had received, they managed by insistent petitions to procure as their co-worker Ingelbert, abbot of the monastery of Fossés, a man of most holy life. Overcome by their pleas and those of their friends, he arrived at the place, accompanied by several of the most holy monks of his house. Among these, two especially

who excelled both in divine contemplation and in all the observances of the holy Rule and shone forth as two great luminaries of our Order: Gauzbertus, the brother of Count Rorigo and William; from their high noble status and the reach of their influence, they had distinguished themselves by honorable comportment in worldly affairs, leading lives perfect in every way. But afterwards they renounced their secular power and, as fugitives from the world, clung zealously to the precepts of the Lord. They delighted in striving for monastic perfection—as anyone who wishes can discover by listening to those who knew them and are still among us. Since, at the insistence of the devout patrons, the buildings needed for monastic life as they appear today had been almost completed at the shrine, the venerable Abbot Ingelbert left behind a number of brothers, along with the two mentioned above, and encouraged them to a holy devotion. He then returned to his own monastery, confident that they would be constant in their pursuit of monastic perfection.

18. So that the monastery should not in later times perchance stray from the uprightness of the path of the Rule through the negligence of its inhabitants, the venerable count acquired a written order from the imperial chancellery of the sovereign Emperor Louis that the abbots of the abbey of Fossés should always have oversight of the shrine. They should with vigilance focus their concern for both the monastery and its community by installing brothers from their own monastery as priors and officials, by whose command all of the shrine's affairs, internal and external, might be properly carried forth. Because this imperial order was carried off and destroyed by fire in Ingelbert's own time, however, I thought it better to say little about it than to expand upon it. At any rate, the men whose names have been mentioned above, along with the others who had been sent to the shrine, first established everything devoutly and honorably within a short period of time. They then, with great zeal, they brought together and united many monks for God through the observance of monastic discipline. By the abbot's order they had also brought everything necessary for divine worship from their own abbey, as well as anything they thought might be needed in a new foundation.

19. So through their ministry, the abbey progressed in spiritual growth daily and an abundant harvest of souls for God continued to ripen there

in the rich soil of holiness. Then Louis, of august memory, conferred upon his son Pepin the county of Anjou along with the abbeys and fiscs that were situated there (along with other assets as seemed fitting to the benevolence of His Highness). Next, by the solemn donation of that glorious King Pepin, possession of this abbey—the story of whose restoration I have been narrating here—was taken by Ebroin, then in the flower of his excellent youth and powerful in the clerical order (afterwards, in fact, he was elevated to the episcopal seat in the church of Poitiers). This was done through the counsel and encouragement of the illustrious Rorigo, so that the foundation might not fall into alien hands and monastic observance thereby be abandoned, as had happened before. The noble count had also decided that the shrine was to be the location set aside for his tomb, for those of his wife and children and other relatives. (Indeed, there he rests by God's will and his own choice.) This Ebroin was a blood kinsman of the count's noble family. So when he had obtained this abbey from Pepin, as he had hoped, and had been made a bishop, he approached the pious Emperor Louis and formally acquired the shrine and all the possessions it is known to have held at that time, in hereditary and perpetual grant, as the famous charter with the emperor's sacred authority, which today is carefully preserved in the vault of our archive, clearly witnesses.

20. Submitting to the wish, and indeed the order, of the aforesaid count, Ebroin granted unlimited authority over this house to the abbey of Fossés for as long as God willed that the noble Count Rorigo remain alive. But after he had died, Ebroin made inquiry regarding the authority whereby the monastery had come into its lordship; the monks were unable to show it to him because (as was noted above), it had been fraudulently stolen and given over to the flames. Therefore he kept some of the brothers from Fossés at the shrine, but the rest he ordered to return to their own house.[6] He did this under the influence of certain men of evil intent, after the death of the august Louis and of Rorigo of righteous memory. He then approached the serene King Charles and showed him his father's [Louis the Pious'] charter, on the authority of which Ebroin held the monastery as a freehold.

7. Levillain suggested that Ebroin destroyed this document: 'Ebroin, évêque de Poitiers', *Le Moyen Age* 34 (1923) 180.

He petitioned the king to validate his lord father's document by new edicts of his own. Freely assenting to his petition, the king confirmed with solemn documents what that great prelate had requested. These documents provided that as long as someone of our progeny can be found who is able while he lives to govern the shrine according to the rule of Blessed Benedict, he and no other may legally discharge the office of rector there.[7]

21. Having resolutely done all this, Ebroin then presented Gauzlinus, a most learned person and most devoutly trained in monastic practice, the son of the holy Gauzbertus, to his Royal Highness and petitioned that he be raised to the dignity of abbot of the shrine. The king—much taken by Gauzlinus' erudition and very learned speech, in which the most noble cleric was proficient—willingly agreed and duly constituted him abbot in the presence of the nobles of the entire kingdom; the king also promised to confer greater gifts on him when the opportunity arose. Once Gauzlinus had accepted the pastoral governance of the shrine, it began to advance nobly in monastic devotion and in his day appeared second to none as regards devotion to divine worship.

22. One can discover from his own detailed account how Gauzlinus transferred the relics of the holy Maurus from the south part of Saint Martin's altar, in back, to the eastern side of the same table (as is the custom in our age). He described the process in this way, 'In the year of our lord Jesus Christ 845, in the eighth year of the indiction, on the fifth day of the week, in the fifth week of Lent, the fourth of the Ides of March,[8] the bones of the blessed deacon Maurus, enclosed in an iron chest, were translated by the servant of God Gauzlinus and other priests into the place where they are now venerated. On that same day, they discovered the relics of the protomartyr Stephen, which had been enclosed for the purposes of veneration in a wooden reliquary next to Father Maurus' tomb by Bertulf, abbot in the days of King Chlothar. These were so whole and without blemish that it

8. The phrase *progenie nostra* provides the only evidence that the author, Abbot Odo, was a member of the Rorigo family.

9. March 12th.

was believed they had been placed there about the same time. During this process, a small fragment of extremely old parchment was discovered, the writing of which over a very long time had become so faded and almost wiped clean that it could scarcely be made out, even by the most careful investigation. When the text was finally deciphered, it was discovered to contain these words: HERE RESTS THE BODY OF BLESSED MAURUS MONK AND DEACON, WHO IN THE TIME OF KING THEUDEBERT CAME INTO GAUL, AND ON THE EIGHTEENTH OF THE KALENDS OF FEBRUARY PASSED OUT OF THIS WORLD. In like manner, relics of Blessed Peter the Apostle were discovered with a small marker set up at his head, covered over by a mound of sand to protect them, as one might expect.' Thus he wrote.

23. The brothers of our community who devoutly attended the ceremonies of the translation of so great a man swore to me that eight persons well known to them were cured of various illnesses on the occasion: three of them were blind, two lame, one paralyzed, and two were women who could not speak. During that year, on the day before holy Pentecost, the third of the kalends of June,[9] the servant of Christ Gauzlinus was installed as abbot, the first since the restoration of monastic observance in the monastery of Blessed Maurus. This was celebrated by Orsmarus, chief bishop of the city of Tours, and two other bishops in the church of the Holy Saviour before the altar that Blessed Maurus himself had built in honor of the Undivided and Life-giving Trinity. Earlier that same year, Ebroin, bishop of the church of Poitiers, had raised Gauzlinus to the diaconate and then Dodo, bishop of the church of Anjou, promoted him to the dignity of the priestly order. Now, however, the course of our story should turn to the distinctive signs of the divine power that were displayed in this monastery through this most blessed person.

24. While the shrine was being governed well and piously by the foresight and the customs of the monks of Fossés and of Gauzbertus and others, happily remembered, a long dispute over the supreme governance of the realm had sprung up between King Charles and his brother Lothair. Since God himself protected him, the serene King Charles

10. June 29th.

carried the day by fighting strenuously with sufficient forces in open battle. At that time, the bishop of the church of Le Mans, Aldricus, commended all the goods he held in a town called Chavennes to the servant of God Gauzbertus and brought them to our monastery for safekeeping. But then a certain Haiericus and his companion Gerard formed an alliance and sent to the abbey messengers who declared that everything the above-mentioned bishop had deposited there would be taken away by force unless the brothers immediately handed it all over to them. But the monastery sent back the message that a clear law concerning deposited goods had been set down by the Lord, so they were prepared to risk grave dangers to preserve everything that they held in safekeeping. The two men then rushed to the monastery on frothing horses, inflamed with anger and overcome by greed. They ordered their men to hasten on and fearlessly break through every gate of the house where the items were being kept, while they themselves parlayed with the monks. So, as soon as the authors of this outrage had entered and begun to berate the servants of God Gauzbertus and the rest of the brothers about the issue, their men complied with these impious commands. Breaking down the doors, they burst in with swords drawn and started to carry off everything.

25. When word of this was brought to the man of God, he called together the brothers and, weeping copiously, he exhorted them to beseech the mercy of almighty God and the speedy aid of the holy Maurus. Then the bells were rung, the relics of the saints gathered up and litanies intoned as Gauzbertus set out with the entire community to a field where now the vine was springing forth from the earth while a most cruel destruction was also occurring. Although the sky was completely clear and the sun was shining very brightly, as the brothers invoked the name of Blessed Maurus in the litany, suddenly a huge crash of thunder threatening terror beyond all measure resounded and so great a flash of lightening cracked that all who had come there, ensnared by the sin of plunder, were now filled with terror that they would perish, particularly when the sudden flooding of an unexpected downpour prevented them from escaping through the gates. In fact, four of them were driven mad in their confusion and compelled the rest to seek the safety of flight. Tossed about from bad to worse, the intruders left barrels and wineskins strewn all over the road, and no one

after that dared to harass the inhabitants of that shrine. The credible witness of the monks, attesting that they had been present, affirmed that all this had been accomplished by the merits and intercession of Maurus, blessed confessor of Christ. From among these it suffices to name only two, Bernegar and Raymond.

26. In that same year, a servant of God named Annowareth, a native of Brittany, was instructed by a nocturnal vision to seek out the monastery of Blessed Maurus for the sake of prayer.[10] After a long journey, he crossed the Loire not far from the monastery of the blessed man. Indeed, two of the brothers who had been sent out by the venerable father Gauzbertus encountered him on the road to Anjou as they were traveling. They saw him at a distance repeatedly throwing himself to the ground in the form of a cross and thought he had lost his mind. (It was his practice to prostrate himself whenever he finished a psalm, just before he began the *Gloria patri* etc.) When they approached him, he explained the reasons for his frequent prostrations. They then escorted him on his journey, showing him the road that led to the monastery. He entered the abbey church just as the brothers were beginning to sing the evening office. He stood between two railings with his head humbly bowed, just as if he were standing before God. The voice of the cantor intoning the antiphon, *The Lord has been exalted over all the people*—for it was Sunday, that great and solemn day—caused him to lift up his head a little. He thereupon saw an angel entering through the window on the south side of the altar followed by a venerable person who had on the robes of a deacon and wore the holy stole properly draped. With his arms extended he approached altar together with the angel. Gazing at the choir, he turned again towards the altar and offered the prayers of the servants of God to the angel standing before the altar. The angel received them and appeared to rise up to the presence of God. The pilgrim witnessing this wondered at it all for some time. When the priest had completed the prayer, the man saw the angel go out through the east window. The deacon-figure then came

11. The miracle involving Annoweaerth is discussed in Paul Marchegay, 'Le donation d'Anouuareth', *Annales de Bretagne 9* (1894) 216-237. Most likely genuine ninth-century documents from Glanfeuil confirm the land donations given by the pilgrim as a result of his experiences.

down through the midst of the choir. As he passed by the pilgrim, he spoke these words into his ear, 'Often do I come here and many times do I thus'. With these words, he disappeared.

27. At once the man fell prostrate, filled with fear, his face suffused with tears. He began to repeat in Latin such phrases as 'Holy Maurus, visitor and guardian of your servants, intercede for us unworthy sinners'. After striking his head on the floor, crying aloud and lamenting, the pilgrim was finally raised up by the brothers, who had surrounded him in a crowd, asking why he was weeping so mournfully and sadly; he replied that he was conscious of the guilt of his sins and hoped by his pleading tears to merit pardon of them from the Lord. Gauzlinus was at that time only a young man—of good character—though later he became abbot of the shrine (after he had received holy orders, as I noted above). He perceived that the pilgrim had seen and heard something important, so he asked two brothers of the community who understood the breton language, Begonis and Winchelon, immediately to ask, in an amicable fashion, why the man wept and carried on so. They approached him earnestly and with some difficulty were able to learn the details of what had occurred, for he revealed to them the visions as he had seen and heard them. For fifteen days the venerable father Gauzbertus kept watch over him, but during the whole time he could not convince the man to partake even of a little wine. When he would agree, no sooner had he brought a goblet of wine to his mouth than an overwhelming lamenting and sobbing prevented him. The servant of God Gauzbertus began to reconsider the case and, deciding that the man had acted that way only out of love of God, he presumed to importune him no further about such things. Indeed, the abbot perceived that the man had received all he needed, so he willingly permitted him to return to his own country. The pilgrim blessed and praised God for all he had experienced, as revealed to him from above.

28. During the time of Abbot Gauzlinus on the feast of the Innocents, the brothers were celebrating the night office in the church of the Saviour. As the abbot was reciting the twelfth lesson (as is the custom in monastic communities),[11] suddenly all the brothers heard voices

12. Cf. RB 11.

resounding with songs of prodigious and indescribable sweetness in the basilica of Saint Martin where the body of Blessed Maurus lay. (This occurred before his most holy body had been transferred from there into the larger church.) Everyone sat up straight, thunderstruck at this miracle and, when the lesson was ended, the abbot himself began to investigate who was producing a harmony of such indescribable sweetness with so many different voices. Two of the brothers, to whom custody of this basilica had been committed, swiftly went outside the church so they could take in what they had heard and understand something of what was being sung. But before they reached the church's gate—the church was positioned on a bluff, so the pace is rather slow for anyone going up the hill—the cadence of the singing had ceased. But at that moment they saw quite clearly an immense light that spread through the entire basilica, some of it flowing through the window and some still visible outside. To everyone it was clear that an assembly of angels was celebrating all this, keeping vigil before the relics of the blessed saint. Indeed, a melody of such loveliness, with notes of even greater sweetness, could be discerned; and very often there resounded the jubilation of a throng of honeyed voices, resembling a band of celestial children. From that day on, such sounds were often heard, especially in the nighttime hours, being solemnly intoned before his most holy tomb, as is witnessed by the credible statements of the most revered abbot Godefridus and many brothers of his monastery, who often testified that they had heard this music.

29. There was a cleric named Manfred, who used to sleep in a little dwelling next to the basilica for the purpose of guarding it. One day, as he composed himself on his bed for his midday rest, he was struck in his side and awakened by a man unknown to him who ordered him to go outside immediately. But he was sleepy and failed to do so. Turning over on his other side, he closed his eyes again to go to sleep. The unknown person then taking the form of Othbert, a monk of that monastery, kept insisting that he needed to lie down on Manfred's bed, as he was extremely weary. The latter said later that it seemed to him that his master Othbert (who at that time was treasurer of the churches there) had laid himself down on the bed from which he [Manfred] had arisen. As soon as Manfred went into the basilica and gave himself to prayer, the little house which he had just left completely collapsed. Thinking

that Othbert (whom he believed he had left in his bed) was dead, he ran headlong to the entrance of the church of the Holy Redeemer. Beating on the doors with powerful blows, he cried out in sorrow that his master lay covered by his collapsed house. But Othbert, roused from his bed, went out into the church courtyard, shouting that Manfred had gone mad. But he was quite sane and told him all the details, pointing out his ruined house. Othbert now understood that all this had been accomplished by God's command or by an angel visiting the place or through that most holy man himself, so that the keeper of the basilica should not suffer death in the presence of the saint's holy relics.

30. There was a captain of one of those ships that sail up and down the Loire for hire, loaded for large profits. He had climbed up the mast of the ship where a line had torn loose from a sail, which he wanted to refasten. He was caught by the thumb of his left hand by a noose of slender cord and held fast. He tried to untie the triple knots of the noose with his right hand, but he suddenly lost his grip on the mast and found himself swinging helplessly. The sailors, milling about below, did not know what to do. They were afraid to cut the rope by which he was dangling, for fear he might fall and be dashed to pieces. Since they could not climb up to help him by intercepting his swinging and swaying, they called upon Blessed Maurus to assist by his merits and intercession the miserable man, who was now at the point of death. Now this was happening just below the monastery of Maurus, on the bank of the fishermen's landing near the dwelling of the abbey's servants. Roused by the sailors' shouting, the monks had gathered together and, with the bells ringing, they implored the mercy of Christ and the aid of Blessed Maurus in persistent prayer. While they were praying, behold, the man who had been dangling seemed gradually to be let down from above! Eventually he stood with his feet on the deck without anyone's help, freed from the tangle that had enmeshed him. The rope was suddenly back in its proper place (no less wonderful to relate than to see) and to the astonishment of the crew, he began to steer the ship into the wind. Everyone praised and blessed God for the great gifts of His mighty wonders, accomplished through the most blessed man.

31. How, through the merits of this blessed man, divine mercy—always the defender of this shrine and opposed to its persecutors, who

presumed by various means to harass the monastery's properties or persecute its tenants—has employed its avenging right hand we have witnessed personally by our own eyes and have discovered by the truthful testimony of trustworthy living men from the rank of monks in this community. To all this we have decided to add a few details. A nobleman by the name of Witcherius, out of the cruelty of his savage spirit, had violently set about attacking some men who had been assigned to the monastery to the extent that the evildoer killed one of the monastery's servants. When this had been announced to the community, at the order of Abbot Gauzlinus all the brothers began to implore the mercy of almighty God before the body of the blessed man, praying that, by the merits of the holy man, the attacker might temper the violence of his vicious impulses and that the innocent servant might be freed from the man's savage aggression. When Witcherius discovered that these supplications had been carried on for some days before the tomb of Maurus, he was struck with fear; that he might not be struck down for his misdeeds, he sent off a man in his service to the abbot and brothers at the monastery, hoping they might agree to retain him in the place of the servant whom he had killed. But he did not thereby avoid retribution of an avenging punishment for this deed. That the prayers poured out by the servants of God might not seem to be in vain, and that no one could doubt the swift aid the holy man brought to his servants through their invocations directly to God and through himself, the divine scourge immediately laid that miserable man low. Those standing about testified that, as he approached his final hour lying despairingly upon his bed, he gathered himself together, and with what strength he had, bent himself back like a bow and sprang up from the bed, horribly befouling both himself and those standing around with a spray of urine and, with a loud cry, he groaned, 'Ah, holy Maurus, even if I made off with one of your servants by killing him, I put in his place a better one from my own service. Why are you persecuting me? Why do you strike me down?' He complained ceaselessly in this fashion for six days; finally on the seventh, utterly exhausted, he left behind his unhappy life with the same words.

32. There was a certain Vulfuinus, a man distinguished in worldly dignity and surpassing many in the order of knights, who during the whole season of Lent had by force usurped the fish tax (which is

called the 'supper-tax' in the provincial usage) from the brothers. He would not respond to the many messengers sent by the abbot and the brothers asking him to restore the tax that was paid to the monks by the fishermen as rent. Finally the monk Gerfred, a man of noteworthy life—who for twenty years had led an eremitical existence abstaining from every intoxicating drink—approached Vulfuinus. He threatened the man with death unless he repented his past deeds by allowing the brothers to receive what belonged to them without impediment. Vulfuinus would not agree and continued his earlier evildoing. So the aforesaid Abbot Gauzlinus decreed in chapter that, when the morning office was completed, the brothers should chant seven psalms daily before the tomb of Blessed Maurus, imploring the mercy of Christ to move quickly against the tyrant. This was carried out with constant prayer throughout the whole of Lent. Finally, on the very day of the Lord's resurrection, after the festive meals and all the other most agreeable enjoyments that the christian world jubilantly and solemnly celebrates in honoring that great feast, the evil Vulfuinus was hunched over the privy in the latrine. A certain Adalgaud, who was honorably staying as a guest in his house, struck Vulfuinus on the crown of his head with a powerful blow, holding his sword before him. Falling headlong, he lay prostrate, still as a corpse, with his privates shamefully exposed. After a while, some of the younger servants carried him to a bed and there, once his senses were somewhat restored, Vulfuinus began to speak, saying clearly that he had endured such things because of his injury to the servant of God. He immediately sent his wife to the monastery and, through her petitions and moaning, begged forgiveness for his crimes from the brothers. When the abbot sent two of the senior monks to absolve him, Vulfuinus told them that he had been struck down by Blessed Maurus because he had presumed to molest his servants. Indeed, the man who had wounded him admitted that he had suddenly experienced a deep conviction that one who had dared to rise up brutally against the worshipers of God should not continue to live. Yet he himself was wholly ignorant of what had befallen the monks through Vulfuinus, having just arrived from Le Mans on Good Friday to celebrate the joy of the holy days together with him. When, three months later, the injured man began to recover, thanks to the constant care of the doctors hovering over him, with his heart hopelessly blinded, he then began to think about how he might avenge himself on the monks for his injury by imputing to them even worse crimes than before, claiming that they intended to destroy him by their prayers or rather their curses. Seething in the madness in his heart, he set out for Le Mans to divide with his brother Herveus a portion of some properties that belonged to them; but—as often happens in such transactions—a quarrel broke out between them and Vulfuinus died, run through the gut by his own brother's right hand.

33. The stable hands once tried to carry off from the monastery by force some wine belonging to the honorable Gerelmus, who had always lived a virtuous life in the house of Abbot Agelwine. Some of the brothers came running; a struggle broke out and the thieves started to attack the servants who were standing against them and objecting to their actions. Abbot Theodradus himself came up when he heard the news. He had begun rebuking their insolence with a mild reproach when one of them, bolder than the others, began attacking the abbot with insults. But Abbot Theodradus struck the man on the forehead with a small relic container which he carried close to his heart and exclaimed, 'May almighty God, through the merits of Blessed Maurus and of the other saints whose relics, hidden away in this capsule we venerate, reserve for himself vengeance and punishment on those who insult his relics and his servants and especially on you, who encourage the evil of plundering by assuming leadership over such thieves'. And after that, the abbot ordered they be ejected from the monastery. Then the ringleader actually commandeered a fishing boat reserved to the brothers' use, intending to cross the Loire. Asverus, one of the brothers, went up and said, 'This is not right: that all the ills you inflicted on the servants of Blessed Maurus were not enough for you; now you're trying to steal the boat set aside for their needs'. When he made no impression by pursuing such issues, he added, 'The boat belongs to the holy Maurus, and you have no right to make off with it'. To him the thief replied, 'I will leave behind for the holy Maurus just as much as I leave for his woman'. He had not yet finished these words when he was suddenly seized by a demon and thrown headlong into the Loire. He surfaced once from the depths, gnashing his teeth and calling, 'Oh Satan, come to my assistance!' Snatched away again by the waves, he appeared no more. Three days later, some fisherman discovered his body between two islands, the belly ripped open and his intestines missing. The fishermen, filled with

fear by the mad shouting forced from the man's mouth by the demons, had taken to flight. Tumbling off their boat, they entrusted themselves to the waters and swam to safety.

34. These few stories should be enough to let us demonstrate the nearness of the holy man to those who attend on him and that he is never far from those who hope in him. But we will, finally, tell the tale of Frederick and his followers—that is to say, his brothers and other hangers-on—men of the same greed and violence as he displayed. They were, every one, the most atrocious instigators of every sort of harassment and the worst plunderers of our possessions we have ever endured. They were all beyond redemption both in heart and action: evil men made still more evil, beyond what the human heart can conceive or the tongue speak, who were, as the saying is, worse than pagans, persisting in every form of evil—especially their crimes of plunder. Still we saw them suddenly struck down and destroyed, as we believe, by the just judgment of God. The prayers, the groanings, and the tears of the servants of God who were so savagely oppressed by those men, poured out ceaselessly before the tombs of the saints and, through the merits of these same saints, were spoken and admitted to the presence of the Divine Majesty. The evildoers were in consequence destroyed by a swift retribution. Frederick, the ringleader and deviser of all the crimes and the instigator of the violence and outrages of all the others, was captured by the Northmen, imprisoned and, as was fitting, suffered an unspeakably disgraceful death. After his death, heavenly vengeance pursued his followers. One by one, they were expelled from the borders of the lands they had so coveted. Some had their eyes gouged out, others lost their limbs. There was Raimbald, reckoned to be the worst of criminals, who could not pass a single day without being defiled by sin, and had for a long time been inflamed by Satan and was harassing the monastery's dependents who lived below the abbey walls. Although Abbot Theodradus had asked how he dared to do such things, Raimbald—in whose depths no christian spirit survived—began beating him almost to death, tearing his cowl and tunic with a lance. Loathed by sun and air and unworthy of living in the common light, he was struck down by divine punishment for presuming such crimes and driven off to his demon companions. Frotmund and Hercanrick, along with their wives and sons and some

of their servants, lost everything they had and were, moreover, held in captivity by the Northmen, tethered with huge iron chains. Thus the Lord avenged himself on those who had set themselves against him and his servants. But Wanilo, a little less cruel than the rest, was freed from captivity while his wife and sons were detained along with others. None of them believed in God or hoped in his salvation or tried to carry through the obligations of a christian's life. In all things may God be blessed, who hands over the impious.

35. Indeed in our own day, we witnessed even more miracles performed through his power as we carried the relics of the blessed man away from the monastery with the Northmen in pursuit. And although we were in unhappy circumstances, we nonetheless greatly rejoiced. We had been delayed for some days in the village of Scamerato and people flocked into the church where the remains of the saint were being kept. A woman, who for fifteen years had suffered from frequent vomiting of blood, came in, pressed by the others crowding into the same place, to implore the help of the holy man. Having taken pity on her misfortune, we celebrated the divine mysteries for her at the altar, over which the holy relics had been placed. Then we devoutly performed the petitions of the litanies and the psalms, as many as we could, and advised her to remain in the church, and in the middle of the night, when we were all, including the woman, deep in sleep, all the tapers in the church—there was a large number that had been set up in the saint's honor—were suddenly ablaze! And the hall was filled to overflowing with an assembly clothed in white. The woman was awakened by their sound and filled with anxiety, terrified that she was about to die. When she began to comprehend what they were about, however, her fear somewhat subsided. One of the apparitions, more resplendent than the others, came down from the altar and approached her, saying in Latin, 'Woman, give thanks to almighty God, who through the merits and prayers of holy Maurus has restored your health completely'. I myself, knowing that the woman was ignorant of the rudiments of learning, ordered these words written down precisely as they were said so that no one could doubt these events.

36. When the woman became aware that she had been cured, she got up from where she had been lying. She began crying out to Gerard, a

man of devout life and a monk and priest of our congregation, who was sleeping between two chancel railings in order to keep watch over the sacred relics. Aroused by her cries, perceiving the shining lights and sensing the very sweet odor, he began questioning her about how the divine mercy had intervened on her behalf. She explained everything in detail. Gerard then came to the cell where I was sleeping and, arousing me from my rest, urged me to go into the basilica. Leaving the bed immediately, I entered the church, and seeing the lights all ablaze and at the same time sensing the wonderful fragrance, I began to faint away. Once silence had been restored, as usually happens, I learned in detail about everything that had happened from the woman herself. She said, 'that perfume, whose sweetness pervaded your senses, filled the whole church just as the reliquary was opened. Then those who had came in began to gather around the urn containing the remains of the saint, sweetly paying homage, singing sacred melodies unknown to me'. The woman's name was Ratburgis: once she had returned joyfully to her own land, she never stopped talking about the divine miracles worked for her through the power of Maurus, and they are praised by everyone.

37. In order that I should have not the least doubt in my heart about what the woman had told me, on the very next night, before I rose to perform the solemn office (it was, in fact, the vigil of the Lord's Day), suddenly I heard voices intoning a chant of unutterable sweetness. But as if a great weight held me down, or as if I were heavy with an slothful lethargy, I completely lacked the strength to rise from my bed.[12] Moreover, Gerard, the custodian of the holy relics, rather strangely, claimed that he too was often overcome with a very sweet drowsiness, as usually occurs in the early morning when people are neither wholly asleep nor fully awake. He claimed that, when he was heavy with such torpor, he absolutely could not rise from his bed (although he often tried). Nor could he see the vision, though it was clearly in view. He said, though, that sometimes when he was wide awake, he could see

13. This passage recalls the Lucan account of the Transfiguration where the disciples 'were heavy with sleep, but when they were fully awake, they saw his glory' (Lk 9:32). The inability to move closer to a sacred vision is also a common hagiographical topos: see for example, 'Saint Mary Magdalene', in Jacobus de Voragine, *The Golden Legend*, trans. Granger Ryan (New York: Longmans, 1941) 361.

some of the celebrants of those wondrous nighttime vigils. Having myself seen and heard these things, I have always—and still do—hold them to be absolutely certain. The body of the holy saint is as often visited and honored by the heavenly hosts wherever it is carried as it is at its tomb. The clearest signs have often demonstrated this. It is only fitting that he should have visitors to his relics on earth who are members of the immortal assembly whose happiness he enjoys in heaven.

38. From there we arrived with the sacred treasure into the neighborhood of Sées. A crowd had accompanied us, gathering together from throughout the area and then hurrying to join us on the road. Because the holy bishop, Hildebrand, was occupied with a large expedition against the Northmen that had been announced to the entire population, he was unable to be present to welcome the holy man's relics or to arrange for their temporary housing. He had therefore ordered the archdeacon of his holy see and selected members of the sacred clergy, to assemble—with all ecclesiastical honors and liturgical accoutrements—at an estate called Merolles, which in his generous largess, the most serene king Charles had granted to Blessed Maurus and his servants by an edict of his august majesty at the suggestion of the holy bishop Ebroin. There, along with us, the archdeacon deposited the reliquary of the holy man in the church of Saint Julian with a fitting religious ceremony. For a year and a half, with great care, we maintained the veneration of the holy man's relics there as well as we could. If anyone could set down in writing how much the Lord saw fit to accomplish through his holy servant, he would, in my view, sooner have run out of time than material. Many blind people, the deaf and the lame, and many oppressed with other illnesses earned the restoration of their health at his reliquary, as I myself witnessed. I have omitted to detail them because I cannot remember then all, and I am especially concerned to accommodate weary readers.

39. One thing, however, I should not pass over in silence: that no one suffering from any sort of fever ever returned from his tomb without the joy of restored health, if one asked help from this holy man in good faith. While I will omit all the other miracles, I should relate what happened to the noble man Orgerius. The man had already suffered from a fever for three months; then for two days he was shaken unremittingly

by its great power. He was delirious and was thought to have lost his mind completely. Then one of his near relations, Count Cadilus, brought him to the shrine containing the relics of Blessed Maurus. But although we advised that he lie an entire night before the relics of that holy man with the confidence of a trusting soul, he resisted. He said that he was aware of his sins and feared that something worse would befall him on account of them. We countered this anxiety with statements from sacred authority and compelled him to sleep there, however unwilling. And to show the sufferer how faith profited him while misgivings hindered, the Lord cured the man of his torment in a single night through the merits of Blessed Maurus! A short time later, the man returned with gift-offerings, filled with a greater faith and now out of danger. Willingly, with the greatest devotion, he watched through the night before the reliquary of the saint. Completely cured, he gave thanks to God and Blessed Maurus that from that day until this he has enjoyed good health without a single infirmity.

40. We were driven way from there, however, through fear of unexpected and repeated pagan incursions, as it is recorded in the letter that prefaces this little work. So we carried the relics of the holy man to this side of the Saône River, where they were placed on the property of Count Audonis and housed with due reverence (insofar as the circumstances permitted). For a year and a half they were kept there, and the name of the holy man spread round the area owing to the well-known cure of sixteen notables. He began to be venerated by a constant crowd of people. Within the first year of his arrival there, he became renowned through his repeated miracles, which would take long to enumerate. Among these stands out most vividly the cure of the sixteen notables recorded above; of these, some were blind, others lame or deaf, while some could not speak.

41. As the preface of this little book fully recounts, we then carried the relics off to the monastery of Fossés and reverently deposited them in the church of Saint Peter, formally installing them there on the Ides of November.[13] The most glorious and merciful king Charles [the Bald], on his return from the territories of Burgundy, was pleased to visit the

14. November 13th.

shrine in person. He asked the protection of Christ at the reliquary of the holy one, displaying the greatest devotion. This occurred on the Nones of February[14] of the present year, which is the 868th after the Incarnation of the Lord, the twenty-ninth of his reign, and the second indiction. Owing to the great devotion which his most christian soul has for the Lord and his saints, the king after a few days sent worthy gifts to Blessed Maurus from the monastery of the blessed martyrs Denys and his companions[15] by means of a monk of particular probity, Otulf: two very precious coverings, with which the holy man's relics might be arrayed on procession days and for the festivities of all other solemn feasts. The king did this to receive the reward of eternal life from the Lord through the holy one's intercession. To this day, he continues so to adorn the venerable tombs of the saints that no predecessor, however famous in the honor of his royal title, might seem to hold higher place in religious devotion. Now, as I rejoice at last in the hoped-for completion of this narrative, I implore the mercy of Christ through the intercession of Blessed Maurus, for I have followed the thread of this history with an admittedly unpolished style, but with a sound faith; so may I deserve to be released from the chains of sin by that same Redeemer and so fully enjoy the delights of everlasting rewards, together with the heavenly host of angels. Amen.

15. February 5th.

16. Early bishop of Paris, martyred with fourteen companions *c.* 250.

A Select Bibliography

Aelred of Riveaulx. The Mirror of Charity. Translated by Elizabeth Connor. Kalamazoo: Cistercian Publications, 1990.

Annals of Saint Bertin. Edited and translated by Janet Nelson. Manchester: Manchester University Press, 1991.

Baudot, J, et Chaussin. *Vies des Saints et des bienheureux.* 12 volumes. Paris: Librarie Lelouzey et Ané, 1935-1959.

Beauval, Jacques Basnage, sieur de. *Historie de l'Eglise depuis Jesu-Christ.* 2 volumes. Rotterdam, 1699.

Bloch, Herbert. *Monte Cassino in the Middle Ages.* 2 volumes. Cambridge Massachusetts: Harvard University Press, 1986.

Boussard, Jacques. 'Les destineées de la Neustrie du IXe au XIe siècle.' *Cahiers de civilisation médiévale.* 11 (1968) 15-28.

Brett, Caroline. *The Monks of Redon.* Woodbridge, Suffolk: Boydell, 1989.

Brunterc'h, Jean-Pierre. 'Le duché du Maine et la marche de Bretagne.' Hartmut Atsma, ed. *La Neustrie,* 1. Sigmaringen: Jan Thorbecke Verlag, 1989. Pp. 56-69.

'Cartulaire de Saint-Maur-sur-Loire.' Edited by Paul Marchegay. *Archives d'Anjou* 1 (1843) 293-411.

Caspar, Erich. *Petrus diaconus und die Monte cassineser Fälschungen.* Berlin, 1909.

Chapman, John. 'Apropos des martryologes.' *Revue Bénédictine* 20 (1903) 285-313.

Chassaing, Augustin. *Dictionnaire topographique du département de la Haute-Loire.* Paris, 1907.

Clark, Francis. *The Pseudo-Gregorian Dialogues.* 2 volumes. Leiden: Brill, 1987.

Claussen, Martin. *The Reform of the Frankish Church.* Cambridge: Cambridge University Press, 2004.

Constable, Giles. *Cluniac Studies.* London: Variorum Reprints, 1980.

Constable, Giles. 'The ceremonies and symbolism of entering religious life and taking the monastic habit, from the 4th to the 12th century.' *Segni e riti nella chiesa altomedie-vale occidentale: 11-17 aprile 1985, Settimane di studio del Centro italiano di studi sull'alto Medioevo Spoleto* 33/2:771-834. Spoleto 1987.

Cowdrey, H. E. J. *The Age of Abbot Desiderius.* Oxford-New York: Oxford University Press, 1983.

Cusack, Pearse. *An Interpretation of the Second Dialogue of Gregory the Great.* Lewiston, New York: Edwin Mellen Press, 1993.

Dalarun, J. 'La mort des saints fondateurs: de Martin à François', in Jean-Yves Tilliette, ed., *Les fonctions des saints dans le monde occidental IIIe-XIIIe siècle.* Rome: École française de Rome, 1991. Pp. 199-213.

De Jong, Mayke. 'Carolingian Monasticism: The Power of Prayer.' *The New Cambridge Medieval History*, 2:622-653. Cambridge: Cambridge University Press, 1995.

Desiderius of Monte Cassino, *Dialogi de miraculis sancti Benedicti*. Edited by G. Schwartz and A. Hofmeister. MGH SS 30/2. Leipzig, 1934.

Dilam, Barbara. *Les Sculptures medievales de Saint-Maur-des-Fossés*. Saint-Maur: Société d'Histoire et d'Archéologie, 1983.

Dunn, Marilyn. *The Emergence of Monasticism*. Oxford: Blackwell, 2000.

The Ecclesiastical History of Orderic Vitalis. 6 volumes. Edited and translated by Marjorie Chibnall. Oxford: Clarendon Press, 1969-1980.

'Ex Odonis Miraculis S. Mauri.' in Oswald Holder-Egger, ed. *Ex Adrevaldi Floriocensis miracles S. Benedicti*. MGH SS 15/1:462-472. Hannover, 1887.

Geary, Patrick. 'Saints, Scholars, and Society: The Elusive Goal' in Sandro Sticca, ed., *Saints: Studies in Hagiography*, Medieval and Renaissance Texts and Studies Series 141 Binghamton: State University of New York, 1996. Pp. 1-22.

Goffart, Walter. 'Le Mans, Scholastica, and the Literary Tradition of the Translation of Saint Benedict.' *Revue Bénédictine* 77 (1967) 107-141.

Goodich, M. 'A Note on Sainthood in the Hagiographical Prologue', *History and Theory* 16 (1981) 168-174.

Grégoire le Grand, Dialogues. Sources chrétiennes 260/2. Edited by A. de Vogüé and P. Antin. Paris: Éditions du Cerf, 1979.

Grégoire le Grand, Vie de Saint Benoît: commentée par Adalbert de Vogüé. Vie monastique No. 14. Abbeye de Bellefontaine, 1982.

Grégoire, Réginald. 'Prières liturgiques mediévales en honneur de Saint Benoît, de Sainte Scholastique et de Saint Maur.' *Studia Anselmiana* 54 (1965) 1-85.

Gregory of Tours, *The Life of the Fathers.* Translated by Edward James. Liverpool: Liverpool University Press, 1985.

Gregory the Great, *The Life of Saint Benedict.* Commentary by Adalbert de Vogüé. Translated by Hilary Costello and Eoin de Bhaldtraithe: Fall River, Massachusetts: Saint Bede's Publications, 1993. See above, *Grégoire le Grand, Vie de Saint Benoît.*

Hallinger, Kassius. 'The Growth of the Cult of Saint Benedict.' *American Benedictine Review* 36 (1985) 195-214.

Head, Thomas. *Hagiography and the Cult of the Saints. The Diocese of Orleans, 800-1200.* Cambridge: Cambridge University Press, 1990.

Heinzelmann, M. '*Studia sanctorum* in Haut-Moyen Age;' in Michel Sot, *et al.* editors, *Culture, éducation, et société: études offertes à Pierre Riché.* Nanterre, 1990. Pp. 105-138.

Hourlier, Jacques. *Saint Odilon, abbé de Cluny.* Louvain, 1964.

Howe, John. 'The Hagiography of Jumièges (Province of Haute-Normandie) (Sources Hagiographiques de la Gaule VII),' in Martin Heinzelmann, ed., *L'hagiographie du haut moyen âge en Gaule du Nord: manuscrits, textes et centres de production.* Beihefte der Francia 52. Sigmaringen: Jan Thorbecke Verlag, 2001. Pp. 91-125.

Iogna-Prat, Dominique. 'La geste des origins dans l'historiographie clunisienne des xie-xiie siècles.' *Revue Bénédictine* 102 (1992) 135-191.

Keats-Rohan, K.S.B. 'Two Studies in North French Prosopography', *Journal of Medieval History.* 20 (1994) 3-37.

Kuttner, Stephan. 'Cardinals: The History of a Canonical Concept.' *Traditio* 3 (1945) 129-214.

Leclercq, Henri. 'Glanfeuil.' *Dictionnaire d'archeologie chrétienne et de liturgie.* Paris, 1924-1953. Volume 6/1:1283-1319.

Leclercq, Jean. 'Monachisme et pérégrination du IXe au XIIe siècle.' *Studia Monastica.* 3 (1961) 33-52.

Leo Marsicanus. *Chronica Monasterii Cassinensis.* Edited by Hartmut Hoffmann. MGH SS 34. Hannover, 1980.

Levillain, L. 'L'archichapelain Ebroin', *Moyen Age* 34 (1923) 177-222.

Machegay, Paul. 'Le donation d'Anouuareth', *Annales de Bretagne* 9 (1894) 216-237.

McKitterick, Rosamond. *The Carolingians and the Written Word.* Cambridge: Cambridge University Press, 1989.

Merlet, M. Lucien. *Dictionnaire topographique du Départment d'Eur-et-Loire.* Paris, 1861.

Michaelis Smaragdus, *Commentaria in regulam Sancti Benedicti*. PL 102:689-932. See Smaragdus, below.

Miraculi et Translatio s. Mauri, AA SS Jan 1:1051-1060.

Morin, G. 'Pour la topographie ancienne du Mont-Cassin 2: la tour de saint benoît.' *Revue Bénédictine* 25 (1908) 468-497.

Moyse, G. 'Monachisme et reglementation monastique en Gaule avant Benoît d'Aniane' in *Sous la règle de Saint Benoît*, Hautes études médiévales et modernes: 47. Geneva, 1982. Pp. 3-19.

Nelson, Janet. *Charles the Bald*. New York: Longmans, 1992.

Newton, Francis. *The Scriptorium and Library of Monte Cassino*. Cambridge: Cambridge University Press, 1999.

Odilo V of Cluny. *Vita beati Maioli abbatis*; PL 142:943-962.

Odo Glannafoliensis. 'S. Mauri vita et miraculi.' Biblia Sancti Mauri Fossatensis seu Rorigonis comitis. Bibliothèque nationale de France, manuscrit latin 3, fols. 393r-407r.

Odo of Cluny. *Life of Gerald of Aurillac*. Translated by Gerard Sitwell. London: Sheed and Ward, 1958; also in Thomas F. X. Noble and Thomas Head, edd., *Soldiers of Christ: Saints and Saints' Lives from Late Antiquity and the Early Middle Ages*. University Park: Pennsylvania State University Press, 1995. Pp. 293-362.

Oexle, Otto. 'Bischof Ebroin von Poitiers und seine Verwandten.' *Frühmittelalterliche Studien* 3 (1969) 138-210.

Peter the Venerable, *The Letters of Peter the Venerable*. Edited by Giles Constable. 2 volumes. Cambridge: Harvard University Press, 1967.

Petrus Diaconus. *Ortus et vita justorum cenobii casinensis*. Edited by R. H. Rodgers. Berkeley: University of California Press, 1972.

Port, Célestine. 'Saint Maur.' *Dictionnaire historique, géographique, et biographique de Maine-et-Loire*. 4 volumes. Paris: J. B. Doumoulin, 1874. Volume 8/2:428-430.

Poulin, J-C. *L'idéal de sainteté dans l'Aquitaine carolingienne, d'après les sources hagiographiques, 750-950*. Québec: Presses de l'Université Laval, 1975.

Prinz, Friederich. *Frühe Monchtum im Frankenreich*. Munich-Vienna, 1965.

Pseudo-Gordianus, *Acta Ss. Placidi et Fratrum ejus*. AA SS October 3:117-147.

'Rabanus Maurus.' *The Catholic Encyclopedia*. 15 volumes. New York, 1913. Volume 12:617.

RB 1980: The Rule of Saint Benedict in Latin and English. Edited by Timothy Fry *et al*. Collegeville: Liturgical Press, 1980.

Recueil des actes de Charles II le Chauve. Edited by Ferdinand Lot. 3 volumes. Paris, 1943—.

Ribadeneyra, Pedro de. *Les vies des saints et fêtes de toute l'année.* 13 volumes. Paris: L.Vives, 1857-1858.

Rosenwein, Barbara. *To Be The Neighbor of Saint Peter.* Ithaca: Cornell University Press, 1989.

Rupert of Deutz, *In quaedam capitula regulae S. Benedicti.* PL 170:477-536.

Sainte-Marthe, Denis de. *Gallia Christiana* 16 vols. Paris, 1716-1865.

Smaragdus of Saint-Mihiel. Commentary on the Rule of Saint Benedict. Translated by David Barry. Kalamazoo, Cistercian Publications, 2008. See above, Michaelis Smaradgus.

Smith, Julia. 'Culte imperial et politiques frontière dans la valle de la Viliane', *Landévennec et le monachisme breton dans le haut moyen age Association Landévennec,* 1986. Pp. 125-138.

Van Engen, John. *Rupert of Deutz.* Berkeley-Los Angeles: University of California Press, 1983.

Vita s. Mauri, AA SS Jan 1:1039-1050.

Voigt, Karl. *Die karolingische Klosterpolitik und der Niedergang des Westfrankishen Königtums: Laienäbte und Closterinhaber.* Stuttgart, 1917. Rpt. Amsterdam, 1965.

Wallace-Haddrill, J. *The Frankish Church.* New York: Oxford University Press, 1983.

Ward, Benedicta. *Miracles and the Medieval Mind: Theory, Record and Event, 1000-1215.* Revised edition. Philadelphia: University of Pennsylvania Press, 1987.

Wickstrom, John B. 'Cîteaux, Cluny and Blessed Maurus of Glanfeuil.' *Revue Bénédictine* 113 (2003) 124-134.

———. 'Text and image in the making of a holy man: an illustrated Life of Maurus of Glanfeuil MS Vat. lat. 1202', *Studies in Iconography* 16 (1994) 53-82.

Wood, Ian. 'The *Vita Columbani* and Merovingian Hagiography', *Peritia* 1 (1982) 63-80.

Wormald, Francis, editor. *English Kalendars before AD 1100.* London, 1934.

Useful Web sites

http://membres.lycos.fr/saintmaur/essai_abbaye.html

http://pagesperso-orange.fr/erwan.levourch/stmaur.htm

INDEX